FAITH BEYOND REASON

Faith Beyond Reason

A.W. Tozer

CHRISTIAN PUBLICATIONS, INC.
CAMP HILL, PENNSYLVANIA

Christian Publications, Inc.
3825 Hartzdale Drive, Camp Hill, PA 17011
www.cpi-horizon.com
www.christianpublications.com

Faith Beyond Reason
ISBN: 0-87509-425-2
LOC Catalog Card Number: 89-62285
©1989 by Christian Publications

00 01 02 03 04   6 5 4 3 2

Unless otherwise indicated, Scripture taken from
the Holy Bible: King James Version

CONTENTS

FOREWORD

When A.W. Tozer died in 1963, a Christian public that had come to appreciate his Spirit-anointed sermons and his always incisive writings was bereaved. In print at the time of his death, in addition to the thirteen years of *Alliance Witness* (now *Alliance Life*) magazine issues he had edited, were ten books:

> *Wingspread*
>
> *Let My People Go*
>
> *The Pursuit of God*
>
> *The Divine Conquest* (now entitled *The Pursuit of Man*)
>
> *The Root of the Righteous*
>
> *Keys to the Deeper Life*
>
> *Born after Midnight*
>
> *Of God and Men*
>
> *The Knowledge of the Holy*
>
> *The Christian Book of Mystical Verse*

From those few titles, the works of A.W. Tozer have explanded exponentially in the years since my predecessor, H. Robert Cowles, issued *Faith Beyond Reason* (based on a series of taped sermons). Other tape recordings, editorials and articles have been mined incessantly. The result is that there are, in various formats, an increasing number of works by A.W. Tozer.

The titles above he carefully wrote as books. Then there were the editorials and articles, less carefully honed but still rich in his godly thought. The tape recordings have also proved a rich lode. Counting audio materials, there are about sixty works out in the marketplace presently. Just in these first months of 1997 I have seen fresh material from the archival collection of Wheaton College and book-length gleanings from Tozer's pre-war writings. A new biography is in process. A more recent phenomenon is the desire of many authors to analyze and systematize A.W. Tozer. A Canadian author is close to signing a contract on *Tozer, The Canadian Years*.

The day when we have fully heard from A.W. Tozer has yet to arrive. As thankful custodians of his legacy, we stand amazed.

K. Neill Foster, Publisher
Christian Publications, Inc.
February 1997

To All Who Received Him

W e begin with an explosive text, teaching as it does about a mysterious, invisible birth—a mystic birth. Here is how it reads:

> He came unto his own, and his own received him not. But as many as received him, to them gave he power to become the sons of God, even to them that believe on his name: Which were born, not of blood, nor of the will of the flesh, nor of the will of man, but of God. (John 1:11-13)

Such a text cannot be properly handled without getting into areas that some may consider radical. It cannot be handled without considering the fact that there are many people in the world who are God's *creation* but not God's *children*.

It cannot be handled without an admission that we do truly believe in the Fatherhood of God and the brotherhood of man. (Stay with me and see what the Word of God says about these concepts!)

It cannot be handled without considering the refusal of many "believing Christians" to accept the terms of true discipleship—the willingness to turn our backs on everything worldly for Jesus' sake.

It cannot be handled without discussing the fact that receiving Jesus Christ as Savior and Lord must be an aggressive act of the total personality and not a passive "acceptance" that makes a door-to-door salesman of the Savior.

And it certainly cannot be handled without a warning that evangelical Christianity is on a dead-end street if it is going to continue to accept religious activity as a legitimate proof of spirituality.

In this text God informs us about certain people being born. That is significant. God has stepped out of His way to talk about certain persons being born, and we know that He never does anything without purpose. Everything He does is alive, meaningful and brilliantly significant. Why should the great God Almighty, who rounded the earth in the hollow of His hand, who set the sun shining in the heavens and flung the stars to the farthest corner of the night—why should this God take important lines in the Bible record to talk about people being born?

Much to consider

There is much for us to consider here, for we generally think of human birth as a very ordinary thing. There are so many babies born in this world every day that it is nothing great—except to the parents and a few close relatives or friends! But the only way to get into this world is to be born. Tales about sliding down a sunbeam or coming in on the wings of a stork do not work. All of us have been born at least once.

Our Lord Jesus Christ was one of the most realistic teachers who ever lived, and here the Scriptures speak about people being "born . . . of the flesh," and as a result of "human decision" and "a husband's will"—the socially accepted rite of marriage and the biological urge that is behind every birth. That is the level of life on which we are born.

No, there is nothing especially remarkable in someone's being born, and yet here is God, prompting an apostle to talk about it. He has it recorded by divine inspiration in His Book, preserved at great cost of blood and tears and toil and prayers for nearly 2,000 years. He gives it to us through translators in familiar English. It is a message that certain people are born, and the reason that it is significant and not ordinary is that these appear of a mystic birth, having nothing whatever to do with the physical birth about which we know.

John says plainly that it is a birth on another level; it is not on the blood level. He says that it is a birth that does not have anything to do with blood or bones or tissue. It is a birth that does not have behind it the urge of the flesh or the social arrangement that we call marriage.

An act of God

This invisible birth of which John speaks is an act of God. John is talking about something beyond the physical birth that we know. The senses can touch the physical birth. When we were born into this world, those around us could see and feel and hold and weigh us. They could wash and clothe and feed us. But this invisible, mysterious birth of which John speaks has nothing to do with the flesh. It is of heaven. This birth is of the Spirit—a birth of another kind, a mystic birth.

Some people are very perturbed when a preacher uses the word *mystic*. They want to chase him out immediately and replace him with a man who is just as much afraid of the word as they are. I am not afraid of the word *mystic* because the whole Bible is a mystical book, a book of mystery, a book of wonder. I have discovered that you cannot trace any simple phenomenon back very far without coming up against mystery and darkness. It is much more so on the spiritual level.

These of whom the apostle speaks had a mystical birth—a birth of the Spirit altogether contrary to any kind of birth that anyone knew in the physical sense. If Jesus our Lord had talked merely about people being born physically into the world, He would never have been heard, and His teachings would not have been preserved in print. Physical birth is too common—everyone is born. But these people experienced a birth not of the body but of the heart. They were born not into time but into eternity. They were born not of earth but of heaven.

They had an inward birth, a spiritual birth, a mysterious birth, a mystical birth!

A particular grant of God

This invisible birth is also a particular grant of God. I know there is a sense in which the sovereign God is over all. I like to think that there is not a child born anywhere in the world whom God does not own as His creation. One of our philosophers has said that there are no illegitimate children—only illegitimate parents. In this sense, even those who are born without benefit of clergy or the formalities of a wedding are nevertheless owned by God Almighty as His creation. But that is down on the level of nature, and it is not what our Lord was talking about when He told Nicodemus, "Ye must be born again" (John 3:7).

This other birth—this mysterious, spiritual birth—was by a particular grant. It was altogether other than, different from and superior to the first kind of birth. This new birth is one that gives an unusual right: the right to be born into God's household and thus become a child of the Father.

Now, when I spoke earlier about believing in the Fatherhood of God, I was referring to the fact that God is the Father of all who believe. He is the Father from whom the whole family in heaven and on earth derives its name. But God is not the Father of the sinner. I do not foolishly stretch His Fatherhood to cover all mankind, for God is not the Father of murderers and the immoral. God is the Father of those who believe. I shall not let the liberal and the modernist back me up against a wall and make me deny the Fatherhood of God.

Furthermore, I believe in the brotherhood of man. God has made of one blood all people who dwell on the face of the earth. All who are born into the world are born of the same blood. Our skin may be different. Some will have blond hair and some black, some curly and some straight. We may differ from each other greatly in appearance, but there is nevertheless a vast human brotherhood—all of us descended from that man Adam whose mortal sin brought death and all its fruits into the world.

The brotherhood within the brotherhood

But there is another brotherhood within that brotherhood. It is the brotherhood of the saints of God, for the fact that there is a broad human brotherhood does not mean that all men are saved. They are not. Not until they are saved—born again—do they enter into the brotherhood of the redeemed.

This is where the liberal and the modernist make their mistake. They insist that because mankind is a brotherhood, we are all the children of one Father, and therefore we are all saved. That is nonsense; it is unscriptural and it is not true!

I disagree with the liberal who wants to reduce everyone to a single level—Christian and non-Christian, religious and irreligious, saved and lost, believer and doubter. I believe there is a brotherhood of man that comes by the first birth and another brotherhood that comes through the second birth. By the grace of God, I want to dwell in that sacred, mystic brotherhood of the ransomed and the redeemed, that fellowship of the saints gathered around the broken body and the shed blood of the Savior!

So it is a mysterious birth, and it gives us a particular privilege. "But as many as received him, to them gave he power to become the sons of God" (John 1:12). It is a gift. God gives us the privilege—the legal right—to become children of God. This is what is meant by a person's being born into the kingdom of God. The Bible actually says that God has *given us the privilege of being born,* and this is not just poetry. Sometimes we use a poetic phrase and a person has to edit it down and squeeze the water out of it as well as the air and get it down to a germ of truth to find out what it means. But this is not poetry—this is theology! "He gave [them] the right to become children of God."

This birth is newsworthy

In the light of so amazing a statement, we can understand why these people of the new birth merited the news item, why they got the byline, why God Almighty put it in His Book that certain people were born in a special way and not just after the flesh. These were the privileged; they had a right given to them that did not belong to others—the right to be the children of God. So it is plain that a person who is a creation of God becomes a child of God only when he or she is born by a special privilege or grant of God Almighty.

It should be of interest to us that this is a right and a privilege that even the angels do not have. Actually, there is a time coming when Christian believers will no longer feel like saluting before any broad-winged angel in heaven. The Scriptures tell us that God has made Jesus for a little time lower than the angels in order that He might taste death for every man. But originally, Jesus was not lower than angels. In fact, God said of Jesus, "And let all the angels of God worship him" (Hebrews 1:6).

The promise to us is this: what Jesus is, we will be. Not in a sense of deity, certainly, but in all the rights and privileges. In standing we will be equal to Jesus and like Him, for we shall see Him as He is. In that day, if there is any saluting and bowing to be done, the angels will do it, for the children of the Most High God have the high grant of being like Jesus.

Why do we not actually believe that? We do not half believe it! If we did, we would begin to act like it, in preparation for the great day. I cannot understand why we do not begin to act like children of God if we believe that we have a special higher right to be children of God. We have a right to be sick inside when we see children of heaven acting like the sons of earth, acting like children of the world and the flesh, living like Adam and yet saying they believe in a new birth by God's Spirit.

How to have the privilege

Now, how did these people get that privilege? They *believed*, and they *received*. I am going to pass over the *believe* part of it because we have "believed" ourselves into a blind alley in many cases. Many who go around "believing" never really get very much. But these born-again ones, these born of the mystic birth, believed, in that they were not cynics or doubters or pessimists. They took an optimistic, humble, trusting attitude toward Jesus Christ as their Lord and Savior. They received Him, and "as many as received him . . . gave he power . . ." (John 1:12).

Note that this word *receive* is not passive. Passive is when I receive the action; active is when I perform the act. We have come to the religion of passivity in our day. Toward God everyone is passive. So we "receive" Christ; we make it a passive thing!

But the Bible knows absolutely nothing about passive reception, for the word *receive* is not passive but active. We make the word *receive* into "accept." Everyone goes around asking, "Will you accept Jesus? Will you accept Him?" This makes a brush salesman out of Jesus Christ, as though He meekly stands waiting to know whether we will patronize Him or not. Although we desperately need what He proffers, we are sovereignly deciding whether we will receive Him or not.

Let me repeat, passive reception is unknown in the Bible. There is no hint of it within the confines of sacred Writ. I for one am tired of being told what to believe by people who parrot everybody else. You could put some of the ministers on perches and they would say, "Polly wants a cracker! Good morning!" all in the same tone of voice. If anyone challenges their line in their books and magazines and songs, they look over their religious noses and declare the person is either radical or touched with modernism.

We have been taught that passive acceptance is the equivalent of faith when it is not. In the Greek, this word *receive* is active, not passive. You can go to any of the modern translations and you will find that they get across the idea of "take" and "took." "As many as took him," says one fine translation, "to them gave he the power to become the sons of God."

An aggressive act of the total personality

It is *taking* instead of *accepting*. Whether you are layperson or minister, missionary or student, note this well. Receiving Christ savingly is an act of the total personality. It is an act of the mind and of the will and of the affections. It is thus not only an act of the total personality, it is an *aggressive* act of the total personality.

When you bring that thought over into this text, the Holy Spirit is saying of the children of God: "As many as aggressively took Him with their total personality . . ." There is no inference that they could sit and quietly accept. Every part of their being became a hand reaching forth for Jesus Christ. They took Jesus as Savior and Lord with all of their will and affections and feelings and intellect. That is why it says in the Greek: "As many as actively took Him . . ."

Evangelical Christianity is gasping for breath. We happen to have entered a period when it is a popular thing to sing about tears and prayers and believing. You can get a religious phrase kicked around almost anywhere—even right in the middle of a worldly program dedicated to the flesh and the devil. Old Mammon, with two silver dollars for eyes, sits at the top of it, lying about the quality of the products, shamelessly praising actors who ought to be put to work laying bricks. In the middle of it, someone trained in a studio to sound religious will say with an unctuous voice, "Now, our hymn for the week!" So they break in, and the band goes twinkle, twankle, twinkle, twankle, and they sing something that the devil must blush to hear. They call that religion, and I will concede that religion it is. It is not Christianity, and it is not the Holy Spirit. It is not New Testament and it is not redemption. It is simply making capital out of religion.

I still believe, however, that if someone should come along who could make himself heard to thousands instead of to a few hundred, someone with as much oil as intellect and as much power as penetration, we could yet save evangelical Christianity from the dead-end street where it finds itself. I warn you: do not for one second let the crowds, the bustle of religious activity, the surge of religious thinking fool you into supposing that there is a vast amount of spirituality. It is not so.

That is why the meaning of the word *received* is so important here. "As many as received him"—actively and aggressively took Him. This means a determined exercise of the will. It means to not deny any condition that the Lord lays down. That is something quite different from what we are hearing. They did not come to the Lord and try to make terms, but they came to the Lord and actively took Him on His terms.

We must meet any condition He lays down

This is the child of God, the believer in Christ who will meet any condition the Lord lays down, even to the forsaking of relatives and friends.

"You are getting radical," you protest. Maybe so, but did you ever read the words of Jesus, "If any man come to me, and hate not his father, and mother, and wife, and children, and brethren, and sisters, yea, and his own life also, he cannot be my disciple" (Luke 14:26)? Jesus is asking us to place our love for Him, our Savior, before that of wife, husband, children. And if we do not, He will not have us. That is the sum of the teaching of Jesus on this subject.

"It is cruel—terribly cruel," you object. The living God demands our love and our loyalty, and we call that demand cruel? Actually, hell is so hot that God is still doing all that He can to arouse us and stir us into action. Lot could have been justified had he forsaken that ungodly family of his and gone out alone from Sodom.

Let us get it straight. Jesus Christ does not just offer us salvation as though it is a decoration or a bouquet or some addition to our garb. He says plainly: "Throw off your old rags, strip to the skin! Let me dress you in the fine clean robes of My righteousness—all Mine. Then, if it means loss of money, lose it! If it means loss of job, lose it! If it means persecution, take it! If it brings the stiff winds of opposition, bow your head into the wind and take it—for My sake!"

To receive Jesus Christ as Lord is not a passive, soft thing—not a predigested kind of religion. It is strong meat! It is such strong meat that God is calling us in this hour to yield everything to Him. Some want to cling to their sinful pleasures. In our churches in this deadly, degenerate hour, we are guilty of making it just as easy as possible for double-minded people.

"Just believe on Jesus and accept Him, and then you can be as you were before. You can do what you did before, as long as you don't get drunk and run after women. Everything else is all right. Amen!" This is the kind of marginal Christianity that is being passed along in too many circles. As a result, we have a religion that is not much better than paganism. I think I would rather follow Zoroaster and kneel twice a day to the rising and setting sun than to be a half-baked Christian who insists on "believing" for salvation and then does as he pleases, violating the lordship of the Savior.

The popular way is wrong

It may be a popular idea in our day to give people something to make them happy and to tell them they can get eternal life and never lose it just by "accepting Jesus," after which they can do as they please. You can have big conferences built on that—even Bible colleges and great groups of busy Christians. But it is an error. The Bible says that as many as *received* Him—took Him aggressively with their whole personalities—to them He gave the right to become children of God.

Shakespeare had Hamlet say, "Denmark—all of Denmark is contracted in one great brow of woe." I would like to change that and say, "All of the human personality needs to be contracted in one great, aggressive grasping for Jesus that says, 'Here, Lord, You are mine, even if it costs me blood and death. You are mine, even if it costs me the loss of friendships. You are mine, even if it means the loss of job or position or standing!' "

I think of the late Louis Henry Zeimer of Toledo, for many years prior to his death pastor of the large Toledo Gospel Tabernacle. Before his conversion, he was the minister of a denominational church. He often told of reading a copy of *Alliance Life* for the first time and how he came face to face with the possibility that he could be saved—and know it. Simply, he gave his heart to the Lord and was converted.

Then he began to preach to his people about the wonder of the new birth and revival came. He was called to account by the leaders of his denomination, so he got up and read to them from Luther's writings and showed them that he was preaching what Luther had taught about faith and justification. They cleared him of heresy, but they asked him to resign.

"That was a promotion!" Ziemer later declared. He accepted the pulpit of a small Christian and Missionary Alliance church (in those days Alliance churches were usually behind a horse stable or over a barber shop), but his preaching and his ministry soon made it the great Toledo Gospel Tabernacle that has sent scores of missionaries—even three of his own sons and daughters—around the world. This man knew what it was to receive and live for Jesus aggressively with his total personality. He gave up everything—pulpit, parsonage, pension. It all went for Christ's sake.

It is time to be men—and women

Why should believing Christians want everything pre-cooked, pre-digested, sliced and salted and expect that God must come and hold the food to their baby lips while they pound the table and splash? And we think that is Christianity! It is not. Such a degenerate, illegitimate breed have no right to be called Christians.

Those who insist that the Lord God humor them, letting them continue on as they are and still say in the end, "Come, faithful servants," are fools. Someone needs to tell them so now!

Revelation Is Not Enough

In one of His confrontations with the Jewish
leaders, Jesus gives us reason to look at those
in His day who held truth to be merely intellectual. They supposed truth was capable of being
reduced to a code—much as we accept that two
times two is four. Here is the setting, the question
and Jesus' reply:

> Now about the midst of the feast Jesus
> went up into the temple, and taught. And
> the Jews marvelled, saying, How knowest
> this man letters, having never learned? Je-
> sus answered them, and said, My doctrine
> is not mine, but his that sent me. If any
> man will do his will, he shall know of the
> doctrine, whether it be of God, or whether
> I speak of myself. (John 7:14-17)

This attitude toward truth held by people in Jesus' day leads us to consider those who cling to an intellectual concept of God's truth in our own times. I do not refer to theological liberals who deny the person and position of Jesus Christ as Son of God. I refer rather to those whom I must call evangelical rationalists. The reason for my concern is my conclusion that evangelical rationalism will kill the truth just as quickly as liberalism will.

First, look with me at these Jewish leaders in Jesus' day. They marvelled at Him, and they said to one another, "How knowest this man letters, having never learned?" It was their concern that Jesus had never studied in the accepted schools of higher learning. Most of the schools in those days consisted of little groups taught by individual rabbis rather than the multi-class colleges we know now. Evidently our Lord had never attended that kind of rabbinical school. So they asked, "How does He get His wonderful teaching, seeing He has never been to the schools of the rabbis?"

Now, this question alone tells us much about the Jews of that day. It tells us that they held truth (and you can spell it with a capital letter, if you wish) to be merely intellectual, capable of being reduced to a code. To know truth, it was only necessary to learn the code. Most people had no books of their own; they memorized the code in school, and this was their concept of truth. We gather this not only from Jesus' answer to their question, but from the entire Gospel of John.

Truth is more than words

They regarded truth as an intellectual thing. With us, the fact that two times two is four is truth, but it is an intellectual truth—proof to the mind. All we have to do is learn the multiplication table up to two times two and we have it. They had reduced divine truth to that same status. To them, there was no mysterious depth in truth, nothing beneath and nothing beyond. Two times two made four. It was exactly there that they parted company with our Savior, for the Lord Jesus constantly taught the "beyond" and the "beneath." But they could never sense the depth of His teaching—they only saw that two times two made four.

It is this that we must remember: those religious leaders evidently believed that the *words* of truth were the truth. This is still a basic misunderstanding of Christian theology. To make this analysis in our own day is not just a matter of splitting hairs. Oh, no! If it were only splitting hairs, I would not bother. What we speak of has both moral and spiritual consequences. They believed that the *word* of truth was truth—that if you had the words, you had the truth. If you could repeat the code, you had the truth. If you were living by the word of truth, you were living in the truth.

I repeat, this is exactly where they parted company with our Lord Jesus Christ. The Savior tried to correct this inadequate view. He showed them the heavenly quality of His message. He showed them that He was simply a transparent medium through whom God spoke. He said in effect, "My doctrine is not mine—I am not a rabbi just teaching doctrine that you can memorize and repeat. What I am giving you is not that kind of doctrine at all."

A new line of battle

Jesus had told them previously, "I say nothing for myself. What I see the Father do, that I do, and what the Father speaks, that I speak. What I have seen yonder I tell you about. I am a transparent medium through whom the truth is being spoken. You believe that the way to truth is to go to a rabbi and learn it, but that is not the truth—that approach to truth is inadequate."

Here is the weakness in modern Christianity, and I am wondering why there is so much silence about it. The battle line, the warfare today, is not necessarily between the fundamentalist and the liberal. There is a difference between them, of course. The fundamentalist says, "God made the heaven and the earth." The liberal says, "Well, that is a poetic way of stating it, but actually, it occurred by evolution." The fundamentalist says, "Jesus Christ is the very Son of God." The liberal replies, "Well, He certainly was a wonderful man and He is the Master, but I don't quite know about His deity." So, there *is* a division. But the battle line is not really on these matters anymore.

Some years ago I went to Gettysburg with friends, and we reviewed again that famous battle of the Civil War. We read the plaques. We looked at the memorials. But there is no fighting there now. I heard no boom of cannons, no clash of swords. I saw no dead soldiers. I only saw where the battle had taken place.

Now in our day, there are still a few ministers waving their bloody words over their heads, but the blood is dry, for there is really no fresh blood between liberalism and fundamentalism. It has been settled; those who are liberals are liberals, and those who are fundamentalists know what they believe and where they stand. The fight is not there. The battle has shifted to another and more important field.

The warfare—the dividing line today—is between evangelical rationalists and evangelical mystics. I will explain what I mean.

There is today an evangelical rationalism not unlike the rationalism taught by the scribes and Pharisees. They said the truth is in the word, and if you want to know the truth, go to the rabbi and learn the word. If you get the word, you have the truth. That is evangelical rationalism, and in fundamental circles we have it today (as my grandmother used to say) as big as a sheep. (I do not know why she used the expression.) We have it among us. It is a doctrine that "if you learn the text you have the truth."

A deadly rationalism

This evangelical rationalism will kill the truth just as quickly as liberalism will, though in a more subtle way. The liberal stands over there and says in frankness, "I do not believe your inspired Bible. I do not believe your deified Christ. I believe the Bible in a way; it is the record of high points of

great men, and I believe in a certain mystic communion with the universe, which is all very wonderful, but I do not believe as you do." You can
easily spot this man. Train your glasses on him
and there he stands. You can tell he is on the other
side, for he wears the uniform of the other side.

But the evangelical rationalist today is still
wearing our uniform. He comes right in wearing
our uniform and says what the Pharisees said
while Jesus was on earth (and they were His
worst enemies), "Well, truth is truth, and if you
believe the truth, you've got it!"

In His day or in our day, such people see no beyond and no mystic depth, no mysterious heights,
nothing supernatural or divine. They see only:

> I-believe-in-God-the-Father-Almighty-
> Maker-of-heaven-and-earth-and-in-
> Jesus-Christ-His-only-Son-our-Lord.

They have the text and the code and the creed,
and to them that is the truth. So they pass it on to
others. The result is we are dying spiritually.

Now, what about the evangelical mystic? I do not
really like the word *mystic* because you think of a
fellow with long hair and a little goatee who acts
dreamy and strange. Maybe it is not a good word at
all, but I am talking about the spiritual side of
things—that the truth is more than the text. There is
something that you must get through to. The truth
is more than the code. There is a heart beating in the
middle of the code and you must get there.

The important question is simply this: Is the body of Christian truth enough, or does truth have a soul as well as a body? The evangelical rationalist says that all of the talk about the soul of truth is poetic nonsense. The body of truth is all you need. If you believe the body of truth, you are on your way to heaven and you cannot backslide. Everything will finally be all right and you will get a crown at the last day.

We might ask it this way: Is revelation enough, or must there be illumination? Is this Bible an inspired book? Is it a revealed book? Of course, you and I believe that it is a revelation, that God spoke all these words and holy men spoke as they were moved by the Holy Spirit.

I believe that this Bible is a living book, that God has given it to us and that we dare not add to it or take away from it. It is revelation.

Revelation is not enough!

But *revelation is not enough!* There must be illumination before revelation can get to a person's soul. It is not enough that I hold an inspired book in my hands. I must have an inspired heart. There is the difference, in spite of the evangelical rationalist who insists that revelation is enough.

These things are happening right here in North America. A minister came to see me and told me of his experiences with a certain church group. They believe truth is enough, the code is enough. Those who come forward and say, "I believe in Christ," are taken into the church and no questions are asked. They are in.

I ran onto a brother who had had a moving spiritual experience in his life, with floods of glory coming down and the wings of love beating over his soul as they did over Christians in evangelist Charles Finney's day. He told me that he had been "invited out" of his denomination, attacked by men whose only accusation against him was his belief in the miraculous divine element of grace. He believed not only in the revelation of God's grace in the book, but he believed that the new birth was a miraculous act of God within the soul.

Who attacked him and accused him of heresy? The fundamentalists did. And the evangelicals did—the evangelical rationalists who say, "If you but believe, everything is all right."

And they did it in Jesus' day, too, when they said, "How about this man? He never sat at the rabbis' feet and memorized the text. He does not have the truth!"

You can memorize all of the texts of the Bible—and I believe in memorizing. But when you are through, you have got nothing but the body. There is the *soul* of truth as well as the body. There is a divine inward illumination the Holy Spirit must give us or we do not know what the truth means.

Right there is the difference. We must insist that conversion is a miraculous act of God by the Holy Spirit. It must be wrought in our spirits. The body of truth, the inspired text, is not enough; there must be an inward illumination!

Revelation cannot save

In His day, Christ's conflict was with the theological rationalist. It revealed itself in the Sermon on the Mount and in the whole book of John. Just as Colossians argues against Manichaeism and Galatians argues against Jewish legalism, so the Book of John is a long, inspired, passionately outpoured book trying to save us from evangelical rationalism—the doctrine that says the text is enough. Textualism is as deadly as liberalism.

Revelation, I repeat, cannot save. Revelation is the ground upon which we stand. Revelation tells us what to believe. The Bible is the book of God and I stand for it with all my heart. But before I can be saved, there must be illumination, penitence, renewal, inward deliverance.

I have no doubt that we try to ease many people into the kingdom who never get into the kingdom at all. They are jockeyed into believing in the text, and they do, but they have never been illuminated by the Holy Spirit. They have never been renewed within their beings. They never get into the kingdom at all.

Now, there is a secret in divine truth altogether hidden from the unprepared soul. This is where we stand in the terrible day in which we live. Christianity is not something you just reach up and grab, as some teach. There must be a preparation of the mind, a preparation of the life and a preparation of the inner person before we can savingly believe in Jesus Christ.

You ask, is it possible to hear the truth and not understand the truth? Listen to Isaiah:

Hear ye indeed, but understand not; and see ye indeed, but perceive not. (Isaiah 6:9)

Yes, it is possible to see and yet not perceive. Paul says, "And my speech and my preaching was not with enticing words of man's wisdom, but in demonstration of the Spirit and of power: that your faith should not stand in the wisdom of men, but in the power of God" (1 Corinthians 2:4-5).

Now, the theological rationalist understands that in this way: He says that your faith should stand not in the wisdom of man but in the Word of God. But that is not what Paul said. He said that your faith should stand in the *power* of God. That is quite a different thing.

Read on from that same chapter: "But as it is written, Eye hath not seen, nor ear heard, neither have entered into the heart of man, the things which God hath prepared for them that love him. But God hath revealed them unto us by his Spirit. . ." (1 Corinthians 2:9-10).

For what man knoweth the things of a man, save the spirit of man which is in him? even so the things of God knoweth no man, but the Spirit of God. Now we have received, not the spirit of the world, but the spirit which is of God; that we might know the things that are freely given to us of God. Which things also we speak, not in the words of man's wisdom teacheth, but which the Holy Ghost teacheth; comparing spiritual things with spiritual. But the natural man receiveth not the things of the Spirit of God: for they are foolishness unto him: neither can he know them, because they are spiritually discerned. (2:11-14).

Paul, the man of God, is saying, "I came preaching and I preached with power that would illuminate and get to the conscience and the spirit and change the inner person in order that your faith might stand in the power of God."

Your faith can stand in the text and you can be as dead as the proverbial doornail, but when the power of God moves in on the text and sets the sacrifice on fire, then you have Christianity. We try to call that revival, but it is not revival at all. It is simply New Testament Christianity. It is what it ought to have been in the first place, and was not.

Now look at Matthew 11:25-27:

At that time Jesus answered and said, I thank thee, O Father, Lord of heaven and earth, because thou hast hid these things from the wise and prudent, and hast revealed them unto babes. Even so, Father: for so it seemed good in thy sight. All things are delivered unto me of my Father: and no man knoweth the Son, but the Father; neither knoweth any man the Father, save the Son, and he to whomsoever the Son will reveal him.

There we have the doctrine taught plainly. There is not only a body of truth that we relinquish at our peril, but there is also a soul in that body which we must get through to. If we do not get through to the soul of truth, we have only a dead body on our hands.

The Spirit brings life

A church can go on holding the creed and the truth for generations and grow old. New people can follow and receive that same code and also grow old. Then some revivalist comes in and fires his guns and gets everybody stirred, and prayer moves God down on the scene and revival comes to that church. People who thought they were saved get saved. People who had only believed in a code now believe in Christ. And what has really happened? It is simply New Testament Christianity having its place. It is not any deluxe edition of Christianity; it is what Christianity should have been from the beginning.

A man will go along in a church and believe Bible texts and memorize them and quote them and teach them and maybe become a church deacon. He may be elected to the church board and all the rest. Then, one day, under the fiery preaching of some visitor or perhaps of the pastor, he suddenly feels terribly in need of God and, forgetting all his past history, he goes to his knees. Like David, he begins to pour out his soul in confession. Then he leaps to his feet and testifies, "I have been a deacon in this church for 26 years and never was born again until tonight!"

What happened? That man had been trusting the dead body of truth until some inspired preacher let him know that truth has a soul. Or, maybe God taught him in secret that truth has a soul as well as a body, and he dared to get through and pursue by penitence and obedience until God honored his faith and flashed the light on. Then, like lightning out of heaven, it touched his spirit and all the texts he had memorized became alive.

Thank God, he did memorize the texts, and all the truth he knew suddenly now bloomed in the light. That is why I believe we ought to memorize Scripture. That is why we ought to get to know the Word, why we ought to fill our minds with the great hymns and songs of the church. They will mean little to us until the Holy Spirit comes. But when He comes He will have fuel to use. Fire without fuel will not burn, but fuel without fire is dead. And the Holy Spirit will not come on a church where there is no biblical body of truth. The Holy Spirit never comes into a vacuum, but where the Word of God is, there is fuel, and the fire falls and burns up the sacrifice.

Repentance is the necessary preparation

Jesus said those who are willing to do God's will shall *know*; they shall know His *teaching*—whether His teaching comes from God or whether He speaks on His own. Now, this body of teaching can be grasped by the average, normal intellect. You can grasp teaching, but only the enlightened soul will ever know the truth and only the prepared heart will ever be enlightened. And just what is the preparation needed?

Jesus said if any are willing to do God's will, the light will flash on. God will enlighten their souls. We want to make Jesus Christ a convenience. We make Him a lifeboat to get us to shore, a guide to find us when we are lost. We reduce Him simply to Big Friend to help us when we are in trouble. That is not biblical Christianity. Jesus Christ is Lord, and when we are willing to do God's will, that is repentance and the truth flashes in. For the first time in our lives we find ourselves willing to say, "I will do the will of the Lord, even if I die for it!"

Illumination will start in the heart. That is repentance—when we who have been following our own will decide to do the will of God!

We cannot know the Son except the Father tells us. We cannot know the Father except the Son reveal Him. I can know about God; that is the body of truth. But I cannot know God, the soul of truth, unless I am ready to be obedient. True discipleship is obeying Jesus Christ, learning of Him, following Him and doing what He tells us to do. It is keeping His commandments and carrying out His will. That kind of a person is a Christian—and no other kind is.

When you are trying to find out the condition of a church, do not just inquire whether it is evangelical. Ask whether it is an evangelical rationalistic church that says, "The text is enough," or whether it is a church that believes that the text plus the Holy Spirit is enough.

Before the Word of God can mean anything inside of me, there must be obedience to the Word. Truth will not give itself to a rebel. Truth will not impart life to a man who will not obey the light! "If we walk in the light, as he is in the light, we have fellowship one with another, and the blood of Jesus Christ, his Son cleanseth us from all sin" (1 John 1:7). The person who is disobeying Jesus Christ cannot expect to be enlightened.

Illumination is a fact

But there *is* illumination. I know what Charles Wesley meant when he wrote, "His Spirit answers to the blood, / And tells me I am born of God!" No one had to come and tell me what he meant. "Those who are willing to do my will," said Jesus in effect, "shall have a revelation in their own hearts. They shall have an inward illumination that tells them they are children of God."

If a sinner goes to the altar and a worker with a marked New Testament argues him into the kingdom, the devil will meet him two blocks down the street and argue him out of it again. But if he has an inward illumination—that witness within— because the Spirit answers to the blood, you cannot argue with such a man. He will just be stubborn, regardless of the arguments you try to marshall. He will say, "But I *know!*"

A man like that is not bigoted or arrogant; he is just sure. He is like the happy Christian brother who worked in a factory, and someone invited him to attend a meeting at which a man had announced he would prove that Christians were wrong. So he went to the lecture. It was powerful and buttressed by every kind of argument. On the way out, the man who had invited him said to the Christian, "Now, what do you think?"

"I heard this lecture 25 years too late," the Christian replied. "It was 25 years ago that God did for me what this fellow said can't be done!" Now, this is normal Christianity. That is the way we should be. "If anyone chooses to do God's will, he will find out." He will know.

Yet some people continue to hold out on God, refusing to follow Jesus, all the time hung up on something He has told them to do, but they will not do it.

You say you are going to take a Bible course. You can take a Bible study course and learn all about synthesis and analysis and all the rest. But if you are holding out on God, you might just as well read Pogo. All the courses in the world will not illuminate you inside. You can fill your head full of knowledge, but the day that you decide you are going to obey God, the knowledge will get down into your heart. You will *know*. Only the servants of truth can ever know truth. Only those who obey can ever have the inward change.

Knowledge is not enough

You can stand on the outside and have all the information and know all about it and yet not be a true disciple who really knows Christ. I once read a book about the inner spiritual life by a man who was not a Christian at all. He was a sharp intellectual, a keen Englishman. He stood outside and examined spiritual people from the outside, but nothing ever reached him. And that is possible!

You cannot argue around this. You can read your Bible—read any version you want—and if you are honest you will admit that it is either obedience or inward blindness. You can repeat Romans word for word and still be blind inwardly. You can quote all the Psalms and still be blind inwardly. You can know the doctrine of justification by faith and take your stand with Luther and the Reformation and be blind inwardly. It is not the body of truth that enlightens; it is the Spirit of truth who enlightens.

If you are willing to obey the Lord Jesus, He will illuminate your spirit. He will inwardly enlighten you. The truth you have known intellectually will now be known spiritually. Power will begin to flow up and out, and you will find yourself changed, marvelously changed. It is rewarding to believe in a Christianity that really changes people.

I would rather be part of a small group with inner knowledge than part of a vast group with only intellectual knowledge. In that great day of Christ's coming, all that will matter is whether or not I have been inwardly illuminated, inwardly regenerated, inwardly purified.

The question is: *Do we really know Jesus in this way?*

Faith in the Character of God

I n our evangelical circles, faith is a theme upon which we like to dwell. No promise of God to answer prayer is more frequently quoted than the one we look at in this chapter. Jesus is speaking to His disciples:

> And whatsoever ye shall ask in my name, that will I do, that the Father may be glorified in the Son. If ye shall ask any thing in my name, I will do it. (John 14:13-14)

Some are concerned because there are not more miracles and wonders wrought in our midst through faith. In our day, everything is commercialized. And I must say that I do not believe in commercialized miracles.

"Miracles, Incorporated"—you can have it!

"Healing, Incorporated"—you can have that, too! And the same with "Evangelism, Incorporated" and

"Without a Vision the People Perish, Incorporated." I have my doubts about signs and wonders that have to be organized, that demand a letterhead and a president and a big trailer with lights and cameras. God is not in that!

But the person of faith who can go alone into the wilderness and get on his or her knees and command heaven—God is in that. The preacher who will dare to stand and let his preaching cost him something—God is in that. The Christian who is willing to put herself in a place where she must get the answer from God and God alone—the Lord is in that!

You must know by this time that I have a philosophy of faith. To begin with, I cannot recommend that anyone have faith in faith. We have a good amount of that notion abroad right now. There are preachers who devote themselves completely to preaching faith. As a result, people have faith in faith. They largely forget that our confidence must not be in the power of faith but in the Person and work of the Savior, Jesus Christ. So I have to confess that I cannot preach that way. I never have, and I never will. I know better.

In First John, the apostle writes out of divine inspiration: "And this is the confidence that we have in him, that, if we ask any thing according to his will, he heareth us: And if we know that he hear us, whatsoever we ask, we know that we have the petitions that we desired of him" (5:14-15).

God is the foundation of our faith

We have full confidence in Jesus Christ. He is the source and the foundation for all of our faith. In that kingdom of faith, we are dealing with Him, with God Almighty, the One whose essential nature is holiness, the One who cannot lie. Our confidence rises as the character of God becomes greater and more trustworthy to our spiritual comprehension. The One with whom we deal is the One who embodies faithfulness and truth.

So this is the confidence we have in Him. Faith mounts up on its heavenly wings, up toward the shining peaks, and says in satisfaction, "If God says it, I know it is so!" It is the character of God Himself, you see, that gives us this confidence.

I must again warn you of the great differences between today's evangelical rationalists and the evangelical mystics—the subject of our discussion in the previous chapter. I say there is a great difference between having confidence in God because of His character and trying to prove the things of God by human reason. We have evangelical rationalists today who insist on reducing everything to where it can be explained and proved. As a result, our faith is being rationized. And thus we pull Almighty God down to the low level of human reason.

I am not insisting that human reason and faith in God are contrary to one another, but I do insist that one is above the other. When we are true believers in God's truth, we enter another world—a realm that is infinitely above reason.

> For my thoughts are not your thoughts, nei-
> ther are your ways my ways, saith the LORD.
> For as the heavens are higher than the earth,
> so are my ways higher than your ways, and
> my thoughts than your thoughts. (Isaiah
> 55:8-9)

Faith never goes contrary to reason; faith simply ignores reason and rises above it.

Now, in dealing with these matters in the text, we
must first go back to the plain statement of our
Lord: "You may ask me for anything in my name,
and I will do it." There is much praying being done
among us that does not amount to anything. No
possible good can come in our trying to cover up or
deny it. The truth is that there is enough prayer
made on any Sunday to save the whole world—but
the world is not saved. About the only thing that comes back after our praying is the echo of our own
voices. I contend that this kind of praying, so cus-
tomary among us, has a most injurious effect upon
the Church of Christ.

Dangers in unanswered prayer

If unanswered prayer continues in a congregation over an extended period of time, the chill of
discouragement will settle over the praying people. If we continue to ask and ask and ask, like
petulant children, never expecting to get what we
ask for but continuing to whine for it, we will become chilled within our beings.

If we continue in our prayers and never get answers, the lack of results will tend to confirm the

natural unbelief of our hearts. Remember this: the human heart by nature is filled with unbelief. Unbelief, not disobedience, was the first sin. While disobedience was the first recorded sin, behind the act of disobedience was the sin of unbelief, else the act of disobedience would not have taken place.

The fact of unanswered prayer will also encourage the idea that religion is unreal, and this idea is held by many people in our day. "Religion is completely subjective," they tell us. "There is nothing real about it."

It is true that there may be nothing tangible to which religion can be referred. If I use the word *lake*, everyone thinks of a large body of water. When I use the word *star*, everyone thinks of a heavenly body. But when I use such words as *faith* and *belief* and *God* and *heaven*, there is not any image of a reality which is known to people and to which their minds immediately refer. To most people, those are just words—like *pixies* and *goblins*. So there is a false idea of unreality in our hearts when we pray and pray and pray and receive no answers.

Perhaps worst of all is the fact that our failures in prayer leave the enemy in possession of the field. The worst part about the failure of a military drive is not the loss of men or the loss of face but the fact that the enemy is left in possession of the field. In the spiritual sense, this is both a tragedy and a disaster. The devil ought to be on the run, always fighting a rear guard action. Instead, this blasphemous enemy smugly and scornfully holds his position, and the people of God let him have

it. No wonder the work of the Lord is greatly re-
tarded. Little wonder the work of God stands still!

Anything we ask for in His name

Dare we realize that Jesus said we can have anything we ask for in His name? John emphasizes that
truth when he says, "This is the confidence—the
boldness, the assurance—we have." I am not adding words, for the original Greek means all three:
confidence, boldness, assurance. The word *confidence* is
not sufficiently strong in English to convey the full
meaning, so some translators have used the word
boldness and others have used the word *assurance.*

It is right here that the person of faith and the person of reason come to the parting of the ways. This
kind of teaching—that we can have confidence in
God and He will give us what we ask in the name of
Jesus—is flatly rejected by the person of unbelief.
That person says it cannot be so, that it is unaccept-
able without the proof of human reason.

Unbelief is not just a mental attitude. It is a
moral thing. Unbelief is always sinful because it
always presupposes an immoral condition of the
heart before it can exist. Unbelief is not the failure
of the mind to grasp truth. It is not the unsound-
ness of a logical premise. It is not a bad conclusion
drawn from a logical premise. It is a moral sin.
People who say they cannot believe in the promises of God cannot understand this language with
which we are dealing here. They say: "We must
have a better reason for believing this than John's
statement that God will hear us and anwswer us."

And yet, all of this time, as the argument goes on, the person of faith is confident. The person of faith does not dare rest on human reason. He or she does not reject the place of human reason, but he or she knows there are things that human reason cannot do.

Not against human reason

I have never been against human reason. I have only expressed myself against human reason's trying to do the things that human reason is not qualified to do. In every area where human reason is qualified, I say, "Turn human reason loose." You have a can opener is your house, and reason guides you in its use. In other words, you use the opener on cans, not to mend your little boy's socks. Nearly every home has a hammer and a saw in the garage or work room. We know what they are for and how they should be used. We do *not* use them to paper the living room walls or to sweep the porch! If human reason is qualified, I say, use it. But there are some things human reason cannot do—things that are beyond its capacity.

Reason could not tell us that Jesus Christ should be born of a virgin, but faith knows that He was. Reason cannot prove that Jesus took upon Him the form of a man and that He died for the sins of the world, but faith knows that He did. Reason cannot prove that on the third day Jesus rose from the dead, but faith knows that it happened, for faith is an organ of knowledge. The rationalists take the position that the human brain alone is the organ of knowledge, but they either forget or overlook completely that feeling is a means of knowledge, and so is faith.

When the temperature outside is hot, we know it. Feeling is a means of knowledge. A young man loves a young woman. How does he know? Does he read the encyclopedia in order to base his love on reason? No, he listens to the ticking of his own heart. He knows it by feeling.

So, along with reason, feeling is a means of knowledge, and faith can be placed in the same category. This means that the person who has put his or her confidence in God has access to knowledge that the person who merely thinks and reasons cannot have.

Reason cannot say, "I know that Jesus will come to judge the living and the dead," but faith knows that He will do so. Reason cannot say, "My sins are gone," but faith knows that they are forgiven and forgotten. Faith simply ignores reason and rises above it. Intellect comes struggling along behind, like a little boy trying to keep up with his dad.

This is exactly why the word *wonder* often appears in the New Testament. "They wondered at him." "They wondered at him, and they all marvelled." Faith was going ahead, doing wonders, and reason was coming along, wide-eyed and amazed. This is the way it should be, always.

Short-legged reason

But in our day, we send reason ahead on its little short legs and faith never follows. Nobody marvels, because the whole business can be explained. I have always claimed that a believing Christian is a miracle, and at the precise moment that you can fully explain him, you have a Christian no longer! I have read the efforts of William James to psychologize the wonders of God's workings in the human life and experience. But the genuine child of God is someone who cannot be explained by human reasoning.

In this relationship with Jesus Christ through the new birth, something takes place by the ministry of the Spirit of God which psychology cannot explain. This is why I must contend that faith is the highest kind of reason after all, for faith goes straight into the presence of God. Our Lord Jesus Christ has gone ahead as a forerunner for us and engages God Almighty on our behalf. It is through this means alone that we may reach that for which we were created and finally commune with the Source of our being. We can love the Fountain of our life, praying to the One who has given us new birth. We can rest in the knowledge that God made heaven and earth.

We may not be astronomers, but we can know the God who made the stars. We may not be physicists, but we can know the God who made mathematics. There may be many technical and local bits of knowledge that we do not have, but we can know the God of all knowledge. We can enter beyond the veil into His very presence. There we stand hushed and wide-eyed as we gaze and gaze upon the wonders of Deity. It is faith that takes us there, and reason cannot disprove anything that faith discovers and knows. Reason can never do that.

Why should Christian writers think that they have to come to the help of Almighty God? They are forever quoting a few scientific facts that, as they say, support the Bible. This is what good men are doing, but they are going in the wrong direction. Many of them are better men than I am, but they are wrong. Not all of the scientific facts ever assembled can support one spiritual fact; we are dealing with two different realms. One realm is reason and the other is faith in God.

If the sun should begin rising in the west and take its course to the east, if the summer should end abruptly and plunge us into the middle of winter without an autumn, if the corn in the fields started growing down instead of up—none of these things would change my mind about God or the Bible! I have not the words to emphasize strongly enough my position that faith in God is not dependent upon the support of any scientific helps.

Faith depends on God's character

No, we have confidence and boldness in God because He *is* God. We have learned enough about His character to know that we can lean upon Him fully.

You may have been told that if you will memorize more Bible verses you will have more faith. I have been memorizing the Scriptures ever since I was converted, but my faith does not rest on

God's promises. My faith rests upon God's *charac-ter*. Faith must rest in confidence upon the One who made the promises. It was written of Abraham that "He staggered not at the promise of God through unbelief; but was strong in faith, giving glory to God; and being fully persuaded that, what he had promised, he was able also to perform" (Romans 4:20-21) The glory went to God, not to the promise or to Abraham's faith.

So, what is the promise for? A promise is given to me so that I may know intelligently what God has planned for me, what God will give me, and so what to claim. Those are the promises and they are intelligent directions. They rest upon the character and ability of the One who made them.

Let me illustrate. My estate consists principally of my books. I have a little household furniture, but not too much and none of it too expensive. That and my books are about all I have. But suppose when my heirs gather to listen to the reading of my will, they hear, "I leave to my son Lowell a yacht in the Gulf of Mexico; I leave to my son Stanley an estate of one hundred acres in Florida; I leave to my son Wendell all the mineral rights that I hold in Nevada." You know what would happen, do you not? Those boys of mine, gathered for the reading of the will, would say in sympathy, "Poor Dad! He must have been mentally deranged to write a will like that! It is a meaningless will because he owned none of those things. He cannot make good on that will!"

But when the richest man in the country dies, and they call in the heirs, everyone listens closely for his or her own name because this is a will with resources behind it. The man has made the will in order that his heirs may know what they can claim. Just so, faith does not rest merely on promises. It goes back to the character of the one who makes the promises.

God cannot lie

Thus, when I read my Bible, I see this promise: " . . . if we ask anything according to his will, he heareth us: And if we know that he hear us, whatsoever we ask, we know that we have the petitions that we desired of him" (1 John 6:14). That is a promise from God! I read the words of Jesus: "And whatsoever ye shall ask in my name, that will I do, that the Father may be glorified in the Son" (John 14:13). That is a promise from God!

Just how good are these promises? As good as the character of the One who made them. How good is that? Ah! This is our confidence. Faith says, "God is God!" He is a holy God who cannot lie, the God who is infinitely rich and can make good on all of His promises. He is the God who is infinitely honest. He has never cheated anyone! He is the God who is infinitely true. Just as good and true as God is—that is how good and true His promises are.

Where, then, do we make our mistake? What happens to our confidence?

We push the living God into a corner, trying to use Him as an escape from hell. We use Him to help us when the baby is sick—and then we go our own way. And after that we try to pump up faith by reading more promises in the Bible. But it will not work—I tell you that it will not work! We must be concerned with the person and character of God, not the promises. Through promises we learn what God has willed to us, we learn what we may claim as our heritage, we learn how we should pray. But faith itself must rest on the character of God.

Is this difficult to see? Why are we not stressing this in our evangelical circles? Why are we afraid to declare that people in our churches must come to know God Himself? Why do we not tell them that they must get beyond the point of making God a lifeboat for their rescue or a ladder to get them out of a burning building? How can we help our people get over the idea that God exists just to help run their businesses or fly their airplanes?

God is not a railway porter who carries your suitcase and serves you. God is God. He made heaven and earth. He holds the world in His hand. He measures the dust of the earth in the balance. He spreads the sky out like a mantle. He is the great God Almighty. He is not your servant. He is your Father, and you are His child. He sits in heaven, and you are on the earth.

Why not more preaching about God?

When I think of the angels who veil their faces before the God who cannot lie, I wonder why every preacher in North America does not begin preaching about God—and nothing else. What would happen if every preacher just preached about the person and character of God for an entire year—who He is, His attributes, His perfection, His being, the kind of God He is and why we love Him and why we should trust Him? I tell you, God would soon fill the whole horizon, the entire world. Faith would spring up like grass by the water courses. Then let a man get up and preach the promises of God and the whole congregation would join in chorus: "We can claim the promises; look who made them!" This is the confidence, this is the boldness.

Confidence may be slow in coming because we have been born and raised in an environment of lies. David said in his "haste," "All men are liars" (Psalm 116:11). We do not read that he changed his mind after the stress had passed, because everyone has a deceitful heart, desperately wicked by nature. We are brought up in a world where lying is a fine art. Turn on the radio or television, and you will scarcely find an ad where the announcer can talk for 20 seconds without lying. We have become used to lies. The billboards lie. The magazines lie. This kind of deceit is all around us, and we pick it up without realizing it. We have lost our confidence in people.

If a man came to my door—a complete stranger— and said, "Pardon me, but because you are an upstanding citizen in this neighborhood, I am here to give you a hundred dollars," I would not take it. I would know there was a catch to it somewhere. We have come to expect the ruse in everything around us.

A young fellow stopped at the parsonage one day. "Good morning, Mr. Tozer!" That he knew my name did not surprise me; he could have learned it from the neighbor next door. He had a smile that you could not rub off. I inquired if he was selling magazines.

"Selling magazines?" he protested, acting as though I had wounded him deeply by my distrust. "I should say not!" But after about fifteen minutes of conversation, he admitted that it would help him through college if I could become interested in a magazine that he just happened to be able to furnish by subscription. But he was not selling magazines.

A psychology of deceit

For the most part, we live in a land of lies and deception. There is a psychology of deceit and mistrust ground into us from our birth. But when we enter the realm of the kingdom of God, the realm of faith, we find everything is different. Falsehoods and deceits are not known in heaven. Never in the blessed heavenly kingdom has anyone deceived another. The dear old Bible itself is a book of absolute honesty.

When Jesus was here upon the earth and walked among us, He used no fancy evangelistic maneuvers. He never said, "Now raise your hand; now put it down!" We have all heard about people who are supposed to be in Christian work, and we wonder if some of them are not scoundrels. Thank God, in His true kingdom there will be no dirty cheats who will take advantage of motherly old ladies. ("You remind me of my own praying mother. Will you pray with me? I need $500 to serve God." He knows she has the $500, and before he leaves she writes out the check, and he is on his way.)

I have more respect for the man who robs with a gun than for the cheating scoundrel who will take advantage of an unsuspecting person with his soft soap and hypocritical prayer. I feel it strongly. If there is any place in the whole world where people ought to be honest, it is in the church of God. I expect to so live and so preach that people can bring their friends to my church and assure them they can believe what they hear from my pulpit. I may be wrong sometimes, but I want always to be honest. As long as I have anything to say about it, any man who is a cheat will never have an invitation to put his feet down on the rug behind my pulpit!

Well, to repeat, the Bible always tells us the truth. God tells the whole story about men and women. He tells us what we would have covered up. The Bible tells us of David, a man after God's own heart, and it tells us how David fell, committing adultery. We would have left that chapter out, but God put it in. The Bible tells us about Peter, an apostle of the Lord. But Peter once swore that he never knew Jesus, and the Bible includes that detail.

Do not misuse the Bible

You can lean upon the Bible, its truth and its assurance in the things of God. You can trust it. But do not abuse it or misuse it. The Bible does not tell you that if you accept Christ you will have peace of mind. It does not tell you that because you are a Christian you are going to relax and sleep 12 hours a night. It does not tell you that you will suddenly become successful or that you will grow hair on your bald spot!

The Bible *does* tell you that you may have eternal life now—with hardship and cross-bearing, but with glory in the world to come. The Bible makes it plain that if you are prepared to put up with the thorns and the crosses, the hardship and the hostility, you can have the crown.

That is what the Bible tells us. It is the good, honest old Book. No wonder God's saints die with the Bible at their side!

"I will do whatever you ask in my name. You may ask me for anything in my name." Asking in Jesus' name simply means asking according to His will. This is where the promises come in: you must know the promises to know what is His will. Memorize the Word of God; let it become a part of your being so that you can fully count upon the merit of Jesus.

The merit of Jesus is enough! We will enter paradise because Jesus went out from paradise on our behalf. We will live because Jesus died. We will be with God because Jesus was rejected from the presence of God in the terror of the crucifixion.

Our faith rests upon the character of God and the merit of His Son, Jesus. We do not have anything we can bring—only our poor, miserable souls. The bad person who thinks he or she is good is shut out of God's kingdom for ever. But the person who knows he or she is the chief of sinners and totally unworthy, who comes in humility depending upon the merit of Jesus, enters in.

We cannot bargain with God

You cannot come to God with bargaining and with promises. But if you will throw yourself recklessly upon God, trust His character, trust the merits of His Son, you will have the petition you have asked of Him.

You can have this confidence in God, and you can have this respect for His will. Do not expect God to perform miracles for you so you can write books about them. Do not ever be caught asking God to send you toys like that to play around with.

But if you are in trouble and concerned about your situation and willing to be honest with God, you can have confidence in Him. You can go to Him in the merit of His Son, claiming His promises, and He will not let you down. God will help you, and you will find the way of deliverance.

God will move heaven and earth for you if you will trust Him.

True Disciples of Christ

A re you really Christ's disciple, or are you some other kind of disciple? To the people who had believed Him, Jesus said,

> If ye continue in my word, then are ye my disciples indeed; and ye shall know the truth, and the truth shall make you free. (John 8:31-32)

We can learn quite a bit from what is *not* said or written. For example, if I say "up," I imply that there must be a "down." If I say "long," I imply also a "short," or I would not have had to say "long." If I say "good," there must be a "bad," else there would be nothing to compare "good" with. So when Jesus spoke of real disciples, there must have been other kinds as well.

Before we consider some of the other kinds of disciples, as compared with "real" disciples, notice the framework of Jesus' discussion with the Pharisees. First, they had asked Him, "Where is thy Father?" (8:19). And Jesus had dared to reply, "Ye neither know me, nor my Father: if ye had known me, ye should have known my Father also" (8:19). Then He continued, "I go my way, and ye shall seek me, and shall die in your sins: whither I go, ye cannot come" (8:21).

A bit later, they asked the impudent question, "Who art thou?" (8:25). Jesus replied in effect, "I am the One I have been telling you I am. Did I not say, 'Destroy this temple, and in three days I will raise it up' (John 2:19). That is who I am! I referred to Myself and said, 'The Son of Man is in heaven.' (See Matthew 26:64.) That is who I am. I said, 'I that speak unto thee am he [the Christ]' (John 4:26). I said, 'The Son quickeneth whom he will' (John 5:21)—that is who I am.

"I said, 'I am the living bread which came down from heaven: if any man eat of this bread, he shall live for ever' (John 6:51). I said, 'I am the light of the world. Whoever follows me will never walk in darkness.' That also is who I am. I speak and I judge, and the Father is with me because I do always what pleases the Father. I am the Spokesperson from the Father. That is who I am!"

Jesus was God speaking

Do not fail to notice that Jesus could and did say, "I speak and I judge. I speak from the Father." Jesus was not in the business of offering human advice that people could take or leave as they wished. Instead, He always spoke with absolute, final authority. He was not just a man speaking. His was not just advice from a good, religious man. He was God speaking.

This, then, was what Jesus told His questioners:

> I am from above. . . . But he that sent me is true; and I speak to the world those things which I have heard of him. . . . I do nothing of myself; but as my Father hath taught me, I speak these things. . . . The Father hath not left me alone. . . . (John 8:23, 26, 28-29)

Jesus was declaring that He spoke for the Father, from whose absolute message there was no appeal. This was quite different from what we hear about in ecclesiastical circles today. A bishop says, "It is to be like this. . . ." However, his decree can always be appealed to the archbishop. But when the Lord Jesus Christ speaks, there is no appeal. It is either Jesus or everlasting night. It is either listen to what He says or be forever in ignorance. It is either take His light, or be forever in darkness.

Immediately someone is bound to protest. "What arrogance! What intolerance! I do not believe Christians should be intolerant!" Well, I can startle such a person a little more. I believe in Christian charity, but I do not believe at all in Christian tolerance. The person who hates the name of Jesus, who believes that He was not the Son of God but an imposter, deserves charity on our part. I think if I lived next door to such a person, I would not put a fence between us. If I worked with him or her, I would not refuse to be friendly. I believe in Christian charity, but I do not believe in the weak tolerance that we hear preached so often now—the idea that Jesus must tolerate everyone and that the Christian must tolerate every kind of doctrine. I do not believe it for one minute, for there are not a dozen "rights." There is only one "right." There is but one Jesus and one God and one Bible.

When we become so tolerant that we lead people into mental fog and spiritual darkness, we are not acting like Christians. We are acting like cowards! We cannot do better than to remember that when Jesus Christ has spoken, that is it!

When Jesus claimed to have come from the heart of the Father, when He was declared to be the eternal Word who was in the beginning with God, who was and is God, we are hearing truth. Our position is clear. It is not Jesus plus a number of other philosophies. It is Jesus only. He is enough.

Christians are not the only "bigots"

We who are evangelicals and conservative in theology are often accused of being bigoted. I can only reply that science and philosophy are more arrogant and bigoted than religion could ever possibly be. I have never taken my Bible into the laboratory and tried to tell the scientist how to conduct his experiments. And I will thank him for not bringing his test tube into the holy place and trying to tell me how to conduct my business. The scientist has nothing that he can tell me about Jesus Christ, our Lord. There is nothing that he can add, and I do not need to appeal to him.

I have studied Plato and the other philosophers. I have never found that Plato added anything finally to what Jesus Christ said. Studying the philosophers may clarify my thinking and broaden my outlook, but it is not necessary to my salvation.

I can only say, let us be tolerant wherever we can be, and let us be charitable toward all those we cannot tolerate. But let us not imagine for a minute that we are called upon to take a top-of-the-fence stand, never knowing exactly what we believe.

An honest person may come to Jesus seeking, yet not understanding. It may take a week or a month, a year or ten years to help him or her understand. But that person can be sure of this: our Lord will never, never say anything but what He has said. Never will He hedge. Never will He put in a footnote, "I didn't quite mean it like that." He said what He meant. He meant what He said. He is the Eternal Word, and we must listen to Him if our discipleship is to be genuine and consistent.

We ought to think with joy about those who are true disciples of Jesus Christ. A true disciple has not taken an impulsive leap in the dark. That person is one who has become a Christian after deep thought and proper consideration. A true disciple has allowed the Word of God to search his or her heart. A true disciple has felt the sense of personal sin and the need to be released from it. A true disciple has come to believe that Jesus Christ is the only person who can release him or her from guilt. A true disci-

ple has committed himself or herself without equiv-
ocation, without reservation to Jesus Christ the
Savior.

A true disciple does not consider Christianity a
part-time commitment. That person has become a
Christian in all departments of his or her life. A true
disciple has reached the point in Christian experience where there is no turning back. Follow him or
her for 24 hours of the day and night. You will find
you can count on that person's faithfulness to
Christ and his or her joyful abiding in the Word of
God.

The other kinds of disciples

Now, what about the other kinds of disciples?

First, we must consider the person who becomes
a disciple of Christ on impulse. This is likely to be
the person who came in on a wave of enthusiasm,
and I am a little bit suspicious of anyone who is too
easily converted. I have a feeling that if he or she
can be easily converted to Christ, he or she may be
very easily flipped back the other way. I am concerned about the person who just yields, who has
no sales resistance at all.

I like the sinner who means business, even
though at first he or she may be standing up, looking you right in the eye, and saying, "I don't believe
it and I won't do it!" The time will come when that
person will think better of it. He or she will take time
to cool off, will take time to listen to and meditate on
the Word. Slowly but surely he or she will deter-
mine that the way of Christ is the right way. When

that person becomes a Christian, you have got somebody!

But the one who is a "flip-flopper," easy to push around, will be easily pushed out again. If he or she can be reasoned into the kingdom, he or she can be scared out again in no time.

Some have become disciples because they found themselves in just the right frame of mind. Here is a man whose mother died recently. The invitation song is "Tell Mother I'll Be There," and he comes forward weeping. People think he is a penitent man, but in reality he is only thinking about his mother. Christianity on impulse is not the answer to discipleship. God will not stampede us into the kingdom of God. The Bible is true when it declares, "Now is the accepted time; behold, now is the day of salvation" (2 Corinthians 6:2), but God does not want people to be helped from their cocoons before they are ready.

Actually, I go along with the man or woman who is thoughtful enough about this decision to say truthfully: "I want a day to think this over," or, "I want a week to read the Bible and to meditate on what this decision means."

I have never considered it a very great compliment to the Christian church that we can generate enthusiasm on such short notice. The less there is in the kettle, the quicker it begins to boil. There are some who get converted on enthusiasm and backslide on principle!

Beware the cult of personality

I have also met the kind of disciples who seemed to be Christians because of the cult of personality. They had been overwhelmed and charmed by a big dose of winsome personality. You cannot deny that when some people flash their broad smiles, their faces radiate charm and people want to follow them immediately.

I have always been bothered a little by personality tests, even though I am addicted to them. Actually, I have never found one that really benefited me. I always seem to come out with a poor score. But I never pass one up if it asks, "Are you a good husband?" "Are you a good father?" "Have you got personality?"

I once confided to Dr. H. M. Shuman, long-time president of The Christian and Missionary Alliance and a very wise Christian philosopher, "Dr. Shuman, no one will follow me. I can't help but notice all of the big leaders with their charm and personality to spare. All they have to do is whistle, and there come the crowds!"

"Just thank God that they are *not* following you," Dr. Shuman replied. "Although they may not follow you, preach Jesus and they will follow *Him!*"

When you think about it, we are told that Jesus Himself had no beauty that we should desire Him. He was not a personality boy. I think He must have been a plain-looking Jew, for Judas had to kiss Him to let the soldiers know which one He was. If Jesus had been a television personality and had looked the part, no one would have had to go up and spot Him.

But when Jesus opened His mouth, grace and truth came out, and men and women either rejected the words that fell from His lips or they followed Him. In either case, they could never be the same again.

The half-disciples

Now, think with me about those who are demi-disciples—that is, part disciples, half disciples. These are men and women who bring their lives partially under the control of Christ, but they leave whole other areas outside His control. Long ago I came to the conclusion that if Jesus Christ is not controlling all of me, the chances are very good that He is not controlling any of me.

It may sound strange, but I have met Christian disciples who were half saved. Please do not ask me to identify them theologically. I cannot. I am glad that God does not ask me to write letters of recommendation for some people whom He cannot place! He is not asking me that, for He knows where everyone is—in or out of the kingdom—and I do not.

I only know this about some of these people whom I see as half disciples: they will allow the Lord to bother them on some things, but certainly not on others. They will obey the Lord in select areas of their lives but disobey Him willfully in others. The result is I do not know where to put them. I do not know what to do with them. Therefore, I must leave them with God.

As for myself, I do not want to be a half disciple. I want my whole life—all of me—under the dominion of the Lord Jesus Christ. It was an old English preacher who used to say, "If Christ cannot be Lord of all, He will not be Lord at all!" Certainly, He wants to be Lord of all of my life. He wants me to be a disciple who will allow Him to rule my entire being.

Suppose a young Christian man starts out with a shining face. He kneels at the prayer meeting and says, "Lord, take me and use me!" He seems to be an exemplary, consecrated Christian man. Then a beautiful girl comes along. She is not a Christian, but she is nice to look at and she has a winsome personality and a soft voice. The young man becomes interested in her, and she starts to lead him away. Eventually, there is a wedding, and they get their home set up, and soon the young man is among those who do not show up for prayer meeting. You ask him about it, and he replies, "Well, my wife had another plan for me." Before long, he is a part-Christian and part-husband, not working very hard at either one.

I do not want to be cruel, but I must be honest. Jesus Christ wants to be and must be Lord. He must be head of and lord of all departments of our lives. We cannot have a girlfriend or a husband or a home or a job shut up in an airtight compartment that Jesus cannot control. If Jesus is not Lord of all of us, we are not real disciples.

Then, there are the short-term disciples

Others are disciples—but only for the short term. I have met some of them. They always leave a way out. They never burn their bridges behind them. They never reach the point of no return. I believe a Christian is a Christian indeed, a real disciple, when he or she has reached the point of no return.

The people in our churches would not be worrying so much about whether they can or cannot be lost after they are saved if they would just come right down to business with God. They need to say, "Lord, I am not going to worry about such theological problems. I am going to face it now, and reach the point of no return. I will not be going back." But there still are short-term disciples who have not yet reached that point. They are part-time, short-term. They are seasonal disciples. They come to church on Easter Sunday, at Christmas and at other special times. They can be very religious in certain seasons.

Have you ever heard of "chameleon" disciples? They can change color with the environment. There are even some preachers like that. They can talk the language of the crowd they happen to be with. If they are with liberal thinkers, behold, they begin to sound liberal. If they were with evangelicals, they sound evangelical. They are "adaptable," they say. "We believe in adjustment." They do not need adjustment; they need God!

As Christian disciples, we should be whatever we are wherever we are. Like diamonds. A diamond does not adjust; it is always a diamond. Just so, Christians ought always to be Christians. We are not Christians if we have to wait for the right atmosphere to practice our religion. We are not Christians if we have to go to church to be blessed. We are not Christians until we are thoroughly Christ's—until we have reached the point of no return, not seasonal any more, but regular always. Then, the Lord says, we are real disciples. We are following on to know the Lord!

It may be well to look at some of the marks of those who are not really disciples. Some of them have a pious look. In fact, on Sunday mornings, they look as pious as stuffed owls. We have some of them in our evangelical circles. People can afford to be pious at 10:45 a.m. on Sundays. It is a most convenient hour. They do not have to be religious to get up in time for 10:45 a.m. church. They do not lose out on their Sunday dinners, either. They get a little fresh air. The service does not last long. The music is good most of the time. It only costs them the dollar they drop in the offering plate.

So, those who go to church only once a week—on Sunday morning—leave themselves wide open to the suspicion that they are only part-time, Sunday-morning disciples. They are not in church enough to prove that they are any other kind of disciple.

They have not given up their other loves

Another mark is this: they have not given up their other loves. Fenelon, many years ago, said, "Give up thy loves in order that thou mightest find *the* love. Give up thy lovers that thou mightest find the great *Lover*. Give up all that thou lovest in order that thou mightest find the *One* whom thou canst love." But these "other" disciples will not do that— they will not give up their other loves. They want to take the world in one hand and the cross in the other and walk the tightrope between heaven and hell. They hope by the grace of God to make one last final jump over the portals.

No, I think not. I remember Balaam in the Scriptures. He prayed a plaintive prayer, and on the strength of that prayer, half the preachers in this country would have drummed him straight into heaven. He said,

> Let me die the death of the righteous, and
> let my last end be like his! (Numbers 23:10)

But then he went over to the side of the sinners and fought against the righteous in battle. When he died, what kind of death did he die? Did he die the death of the righteous? I say no. He died the death of the sinner because he had lived the life of a sinner. The person who wants to die the death of the righteous must live the life of the righteous. The person who wants to die a Christian must live a Christian. The person who wants the Advocate above to be a shelter for him or her in that hour must allow Him to be a shelter right now!

Still some other marks

Do you want to know another mark of the "other" disciples? Well, they will always be attracted to their own crowd. They will always go their own company. In most churches there are some who claim to be disciples who have scarcely attended a prayer meeting a year. Some time ago Dr. William Pettengil spelled it out for us. He was preaching from the Acts, and he came to the passage, "And being let go, [Peter and John] went to their own company" (4:23). Dr. Pettengil bore down rather hard on the fact that all of us human beings, if free to do so, generally gravitate to our own company. Let some people go, and they will soon be fishing with other fishermen. Let another group go, and before long they will be in a music hall listening to an opera. Let others go and you will soon find them sitting at the race track watching the horses. Christians flock together, too. Those who have a prayer meeting heart will be at the prayer meeting. If we have Christian hearts, we will be more than Sunday morning Christians.

There are also those who say, "I am a disciple of Christ," but they flippantly ignore—or reject— many of His words and commandments.

Some teachers have tried to enshroud Jesus in a pink fog of sentimentality. But there is really no excuse for misunderstanding Him. He drew the line as taut as a violin string. He said, "He that is not with me is against me; and he that gathereth not with me scattereth abroad" (Matthew 12:30). "But he that believeth not is condemned already, because he hath not believed in the name of the only begotten Son of God" (John 3:18). "And he that believeth not the Son shall not see life; but the wrath of

God abideth on him" (John 3:36). At that great day when He judges mankind, Jesus says He "shall separate them one from another, as a shepherd divideth his sheep from the goats." The one group "shall go away into everlasting punishment: but the righteous into life eternal" (Matthew 25:32, 46). Those statements leave no twilight zone, no in-between.

Consider the benefits promised to the true disciples. Jesus said, "And ye shall know the truth, and the truth shall make you free" (John 8:32). No one can know truth except the one who obeys truth. You think you know truth. People memorize the Scriptures by the yard, but that is not a guarantee of knowing the truth. Truth is not a text. Truth is in the text, but it takes the text plus the Holy Spirit to bring truth to a human soul. A person can memorize a text, but the truth must come from the Holy Spirit through the text. Faith comes by hearing the Word, but faith is also the gift of God by the Holy Spirit.

Truth requires inward illumination

Truth must be understood by inward illumination. Then we know the truth. Until that time, we do not know it. That is why Jesus said, "If ye continue in my word"—that is, if you continue in My teachings—"then are ye my disciples indeed; And ye shall know the truth, and the truth shall make you free" (John 8:31-32).

I heard through missionaries of a boy overseas who had memorized Jesus' entire Sermon on the Mount. He did it in such record time and with such apparently little effort that someone called him in to find out how he had done it.

"Well," said the boy, "I would memorize a verse and then trust God to help me put it into practice. Then I would memorize the next verse and say, 'Lord, help me to live this one, too.'" The boy said that in that fashion he had memorized the entire Sermon on the Mount.

That boy had truth on his side. He did not consider truth to be something objective, simply to be filed in the mind as knowledge. Rather, truth to him was also subjective—to be acted on. Truth becomes real to us within our beings by obedience and faith.

Charles G. Finney taught that it was wrong—morally wrong—to teach objective doctrine without a moral application. I have gone to Bible classes and listened to men who were learned in the Word of God. Still I have come away as cold as a pickled fish. There was no help, no lift in my spirit, nothing to warm the inside of my heart. The truth had been given to me just like a proposition in Euclid or a mathematical formula from Pythagoras. And the answer is, "So what? Let's go and have a soda!" Are we aware that we can give people objective truth without moral application? If God's moral Word is true, it means us. And if it means us, we ought to obey it. That is life. That is knowing the truth.

And the other benefits?

Not only can we know truth, but the truth makes us free. How we long for that benefit! There is a doxology to Jesus in the Revelation that reads like this:

> Unto him that loved us, and *washed* us from our sins in his own blood, And hath made us kings and priests unto God and his Father; to him be glory and dominion for ever and ever. Amen. (Revelation 1:5-7, emphasis added)

Notice the word *washed*. What does a laundry do with our clothes? Our contacts with civilization make our clothes dirty, greasy, sometimes spotted. The dirt is not only on our clothes; soon it is actually *in* them. We can shake the garment, argue with it, talk to it, read Shakespeare to it, lecture it on patriotism or the advances of civilization. Still it is soiled and dirty. The dirt must be loosed. The garment but be set free from its soil.

At the laundry the garment is immersed in a solution that looses the dirt. Then it is rinsed, dried, pressed and sent back to its wearer, clean and presentable. But it had to undergo a process that would free it from the dirt.

The only solution that will loose us from our sins is the blood of Jesus Christ. He loved us and freed us—washed us—from our sins in His own blood. Education, refinement—nothing else worked. But when Jesus' blood did its work, we were free!

"And ye shall know the truth," Jesus said, "and the truth shall make you free" (John 8:32). The truth will lead you to the cross, to the Lamb, to the fountain filled with blood, and you will be free from your sins. But there must be a moral commitment. If there is not, there is no understanding. If there is no understanding, there is no cleansing.

Are you obeying the truth as it is revealed by the Spirit of God? Are you enjoying the benefits of freedom in Jesus Christ? Are you one of His *true* disciples?

Conscience Isolates Every Person

I n this generation, a minister of the gospel can scarcely be popular in the pulpit if he bears down hard on the subject of conscience.

What is happening to us in the Christian church that we no longer believe in the human conscience? God has given us a faithful witness inside our own beings—a witness able to single each of us out and reveal our loneliness—the loneliness of the individual in a vast, unexplored universe destined to meet an angry God. That is the terror of the conscience.

Why should the church be afraid to admit to conscience when the Word of God has much to say about it? The Bible reminds us that conscience is always on God's side. It judges conduct in the light of the moral law, "while accusing or else excusing," as the Bible says (Romans 2:15).

Once as guest speaker I preached on the conscience, and after the message an elderly brother took me aside and said he had become greatly burdened for me as a minister because of my sermon. Obviously, he did not believe in the human conscience. Another man, a notable among evangelicals, also came up to me. He, too, felt that conscience was not important.

Satan by his propaganda has brought into disrepute many of life's verities, including the conscience. When conscience is mentioned now in learned circles, it is mentioned only with a smirk. That is one way the devil has of getting rid of things—getting us humans to make jokes about them. It is part of the process by which the mind is corrupted, for whenever any humor takes holy things for its object, that humor is devilish.

In our day Christians are fast becoming sacrilegious jokesters. They joke about death and life. They joke about prayer and God. And they joke about the conscience. It has come to the point where we must defend the whole concept of human conscience if we are to speak of it seriously. That seems almost unbelievable, but it is true.

The Light that lights every person who comes into the world is not a joking matter. That Light which God has set within the human breast, which can isolate a soul and hang it between heaven and hell, as lonely as if God had created but that one person—that is not a joking matter. Joke about politics if you must joke. Politics is usually funny anyway. But do not joke about God, and do not joke about conscience.

A universal concept

I cannot ignore what the universal wisdom of the race has recognized—the idea of a conscience within the heart of each person. The human conscience is the universal testimony of all peoples in all ages. Neither will I defend what the Scriptures take for granted and in some instances clearly teach. If you will go through your Bible concordance, you will find conscience mentioned in a number of places. And the idea that the word *conscience* embodies is mentioned throughout the Bible. It underlies the whole structure of the Scriptures and is woven into the entire revelation.

I want to tell you what I mean by conscience, and then point to biblical examples of its operation. Finally, I want to show what it has done and is doing to people today.

By conscience I mean that which always refers to right and wrong. Conscience is never concerned with theories. Conscience is always concerned with right and wrong and with the relation of the individual to that which is right or wrong.

In this connection, I notice an interesting fact. The conscience never deals in plurals but always in the singular. There is only one place in the entire Bible where conscience is used in the plural, and that is where Paul wrote to Christians in Corinth saying he commended himself to their consciences. Everywhere else it is referred to in the singular, and always conscience in the Bible refers to right and wrong. So it is individual and exclusive. It never permits plurals; it excludes everyone else and never lets a person lean on another. Conscience singles a person out as though no one else existed.

The word *conscience* in the Scriptures refers to moral sight. It means to see completely; it means an inward awareness; it means to be secretly aware of. That is the psychological definition of conscience.

But there is also a ground of conscience, and that is what we are concerned with here more than with a psychological definition. That ground of human conscience, I believe, is the secret presence of Christ in the world. Christ is in the world, and His secret presence is the ground of human conscience. It is a moral awareness.

"The true Light which lighteth"

A verse I quote often is basic to my theology of conscience: " . . . the true Light which lighteth every man that cometh into the world" (John 1:9). In fact, that Light has come into the world—Light that lights every person who also comes into the world. That Light is the ground of moral conscience. However it operates, that is its ground. That is why it is here. The living, eternal Word is present in the world, present in human society—secretly present. Thus humanity has a secret awareness of moral values.

I know there are some who contend that when the Bible says we are "dead in [our] trespasses and sins" (Ephesians 2:1), it means we are dead in such a literal sense of the word that we have no moral awareness. They say we are like corpses until God in His sovereign mercy raises us from the dead through the new birth. Then we are prepared to listen. That kind of exegesis is faulty. It should be rejected immediately. It has no place at all in the Scriptures. Simply because the Bible says we are dead in trespasses and sins, it does not follow that we are just dead lumps that cannot be talked to, persuaded, convicted, convinced, pleaded with, frightened, appealed to.

When the Bible says we are dead in trespasses and sins, it means that we are cut off from the life of God, and that is all that it means. Of course, that in itself is so bad that it is impossible to think of anything worse. But within that same person who is cut off from the life of God and dead in sins, is a moral awareness. He or she has a secret inner voice that is always talking to him or her—the Light that lights every person who comes into the world. It is a singular voice in the bosom of every human being, accusing or even defending him or her, as Paul explains it. That is what I mean by conscience.

In John 8 we have an example of the operation of the human conscience. Those Jews of Jesus' day were very strict moralists, particularly when others were watching. They were not strict when they could get away with something in private. These teachers of the law and Pharisees had apprehended a poor wretched women in the act of adultery. They had no underlying compassion or concern about the woman or about the broken law or about the spiritual welfare of Israel. They really had only one thing in mind.

They wanted to silence Jesus

The one purpose of these Jewish leaders was to deal with this religious Teacher who was embarrassing them. They were going to silence Him for good. They would get Him to commit Himself to a statement they could use against Him. Then they would take the hide off Him. They would drive Him out with loss of face, discredited forever. That was their agenda and their plot. The woman was merely a pawn, nothing more. They had no love for her as a person, and they had no hatred of her sin. It was Jesus whom they hated, and they would do anything to get at Him.

So they dragged this poor miserable woman into Jesus' presence and said to Him in effect: "Here is a harlot, caught in the act. The law of Moses says we are to stone her to death. What do you say?"

If Jesus had answered, "Stone her to death," and if they had done so, the Romans would have put Jesus in prison and that would be the end of Him. If He said, "Let her go," they could reply, "We always knew you were against the law of Moses," and that would be the end of Him as a teacher in Israel. He would be completely discredited before the law.

I must admit that I have always taken considerable personal delight in the way Jesus handled these His countrymen. He knew their hypocrisy. He knew they had no compassion or concern for the woman. He knew that they had no basic concern for the law. He knew they hated Him, and He perceived the trap they had set. Not only that, He knew their false piety, their phylacteries, their long robes, their sanctimonious looks and, above all, their pseudo-spirituality and artificial godliness.

So the Jews persisted: "All right, Teacher, we are supposed to stone her. What do you say?"

I have wondered if there might have been a trace of a knowing twinkle in Jesus' eyes as He looked at those adversaries and then challenged them individually and as a group: "He that is without sin among you, let him first cast a stone at her" (John 8:7). Then, disregarding them, Jesus stooped and wrote something on the ground with His finger. Being smitten by that inner voice, the men began to sneak out.

Conscience convicted them

One left, ashamed to say anything to the man next to him. Then the next and the next until each one, of his own initiative, had slipped out quietly. It is in the power of conscience to isolate the human soul and take away all of its helps and encouragements.

Some of those pious old fellows thought that because they were old and had forgotten their early sins, God had forgotten them also. But as soon as the voice of Jesus roused them within, they remembered, and they sneaked out. They went out, afraid to look up, perhaps for fear that God would start throwing stones at them, for they knew they were just as guilty as the woman they had brought before Jesus.

The law of Moses that decreed death to the adulterer was meant for holy people, not for the wicked. It was never meant that one sinner should put another sinner to death. It was never thus meant, and Jesus knew it. When these old hypocrites ran into Jesus, it was like a cat running into a mowing machine. Every one of them went away licking his wounds. Each one was ashamed.

That is how conscience works. It smites the inner life, it touches the heart, it isolates us—sets us off all by ourselves. To my mind, that is what will put the dread in judgment—that each person must go alone—alone in the universe before the bar of God. That is exactly what the conscience does: it singles a person out.

So God has given us a faithful witness within our own beings. I believe that. Conscience-stricken, smitten inside, hit by a stroke from heaven, each man, one by one, sneaked away. That is what conscience does. It is an inner voice that talks inside a person. It is one voice that we all have heard.

Some people wish they could have lived in Jesus' day so they could have heard His voice and His teaching. They forget there were thousands who heard Jesus but who had no idea what He was talking about. They forget that His own disciples had to wait for the Holy Spirit at Pentecost to know what He had been telling them. *If only I had heard Jesus,* you may have said. No, you are better off now. You have the Light that lights every person. You have the voice of the inner conscience.

Some are sorry they never heard Dwight L. Moody or Albert B. Simpson in person. But I remind you that even if we could have the apostle Paul on magnetic tape—even if he were preaching in our midst—his speech could do no more for us than the Holy Spirit can do with the Bible and the human conscience.

A truer voice

We have heard a truer voice than Simpson's or Moody's. We have heard a more wonderful voice than Paul's. We have heard *the* Voice—the first Voice and the last Voice. We have heard the Voice of the Light within the heart, the Voice that those accusers of the woman heard.

It is sheer hypocrisy to say, "If only I could have heard the greatest preachers!" Congregations of half-saved Christians pay no attention to the Light in their midst—the Light that lights every person. They ignore the Voice that sounds within them. The Church needs to listen to the inner Voice and do something about His message!

I do not wish to detract from the great men of the ministry. But they are not the answer to our needs. Do not forget that Paul had his hypocrites, Peter his Ananiases and Sapphiras, Jesus His Judas. The great preachers and great evangelists did not have 100 percent success. Always there were those who heard their voices and yet did not know what they were hearing. You are hearing a more eloquent

word than mine; you are hearing a word more serious than that of any preacher or writer.

In New York City I once joined a small group at-
tending a noon-day service. The minister said
something I cannot forget. He said, "We assume
that if a person has heard the gospel, he or she has
been enlightened. But it is a false assumption. Just
to have heard a man preach the Scriptures does not
necessarily mean that he or she has been enlightened."

No, it is not the voice that enlightens. It is the
Holy Spirit, the point of contact. It is the Spirit of
God speaking within. It is that which illuminates a
person and makes him or her accountable to God.
The words of a text falling on the human ear may
not mean anything. That inner Voice means everything! A person has not been illuminated until that
inner Voice begins to sound within him or her, and
that Voice is the Voice of conscience, the Voice of
conviction.

What people do to their consciences

Next, we want to notice what people do to their
consciences. The apostle Paul told Timothy that the
goal of the younger man's pastoral oversight
should be ". . . charity out of a pure heart, and of a
good conscience, and of faith unfeigned" (1 Timothy 1:5). Some, Paul adds, "from which some having swerved" from heart purity, a good conscience
and sincere faith and have "turned aside unto vain
jangling" (1:6). Clearly, then, some people do have a
good conscience, while others, like stubborn horses,

have turned away from a good conscience. They would not listen to their conscience, and, as a result, their religion has become just "vain jangling." They are the Christians who find it possible to live carelessly. But there is a penalty for careless living, whether we know it or not. Think of these victims who are now the meaningless talkers. They vocalize just as loudly as ever about religion, but it is merely talk because they have put away a good conscience. All the sermons in the world will be wasted if there is not a good, clear conscience. Such as these are not able to receive and respond to the truth.

Paul had other counsel for Timothy that related to the conscience. He mentions certain teachers who "some shall depart from the faith, giving heed to seducing spirits, and doctrines of devils" (1 Timothy 4:1). He says, "Speaking lies in hypocrisy; having their conscience seared with a hot iron" (4:2).

You should know that these who have the seared consciences fall away into false doctrine. We wonder how it is that a person who has been brought up in the Word of truth suddenly can turn away from it into some false religion. You may say, "He or she became confused." No. False doctrine can have no power upon a good conscience. But when a conscience has been seared, when a person has played with fire and burned his or her conscience, searing it until he or she can handle the hot iron of sin without cringing, then there is no longer any safety for that person. The man or woman can go off into strange cults, into heresy, into any one of the false religions.

Why is it that people reared in Sunday school, who learned the Ten Commandments, knew the Sermon on the Mount and could recite the story of Christ's birth and crucifixion and resurrection will turn to one of the many false cults rampant in our land? The answer is that they fooled with the inner voice and would not listen to the sound of the preacher within them. God turned from them and let them go. With a seared conscience they wandered into the arms of a false religion.

"Defiled" consciences

There are still others, Paul told Titus, who are living with "defiled" consciences. "But even their mind and conscience is defiled," he says. "They profess that they know God; but in works they deny him, being abominable, and disobedient, and unto every good work reprobate" (Titus 1:15-16). These are people who are defiled inwardly. Even their language is soiled. I am just as afraid of people with soiled tongues as I am of those with a communicable disease. A soiled, filthy tongue is evidence of a deeper disease that has stilled the conscience.

When our boys were growing up, we were always concerned, like all parents, about the illnesses and diseases of childhood. Once when one of the boys became ill, I was afraid that it was scarlet fever. I dashed off to the library and hurried to the medical section. I soon read that scarlet fever has one telltale symptom: the "strawberry" tongue! So I went back home and examined my boy's tongue. It was not "strawberry," and he did not have scarlet fever.

But I had been frightened. That strawberry tongue is the evidence of a million destructive microbes within the body.

But when I find the defiled tongue in a human head, it is a symptom of a different kind of disease. I do not care if it has just finished preaching a sermon. I do not care if it has prayed for an hour. If the possessor of that tongue can go around the corner to the drug store and use defiled language in his or her conversation, I am afraid of that person! He or she surely has a disease; his or her conscience is defiled.

These people end up "unto every good work reprobate," Titus 1:16 says. I do not like that word *reprobate*. It conveys the idea of someone who has been washed up—a moral shipwreck. It is someone who has been washed up on the beach, beaten by the sand, baked by the sun and whipped by the wind until no one wants him or her any more. Paul said to the Corinthian Christians, "But I keep under my body, and bring it into subjection: lest that by any means, when I have preached to others, I myself should be a castaway" (1 Corinthians 9:27). He did not want to be spiritually unfit. And neither do I.

The "sprinkled" conscience

I must mention one other type of conscience—one I mention thankfully. It is the "sprinkled" conscience. The writer to the Hebrews recommends that we have "our hearts sprinkled from an evil conscience" (10:22). One of the most relieving, enriching, wholesome, wondrous things in the wide world is that sense of liberation when the conscience goes free! When God gives freedom to the laboring conscience, the heart suddenly knows itself clean, and the burden lifts. Even the mind is set free. There comes the knowledge that heaven is pleased, that God is smiling and that sins are gone. This, indeed, is one of the most wonderful experiences in all the world—a conscience sprinkled with the cleansing blood of Calvary!

A diseased, smarting, protesting evil conscience lies burdened and heavy until God sprinkles it. Suddenly it is clean in the blood of the Lamb. Until that time, you can go to a priest, who will give you absolution, but he has only buried your conscience under a little religion. If you are ever going to get right with God, all these sins must be confessed.

A fellow told me that he had confessed his sins many times and had received absolution. But before he could get converted, God had to forgive him all over again! That is what he told me. When once those sins are really cleansed and forgiven, a person knows it. Within each of us is a voice accusing us or excusing us. And when once that voice says "Peace!" and we have the "answer of a good conscience toward God" (1 Peter 3:21), we can get up and know that everything is right. No one in the world can make us downhearted then! That is the kind of conversion I believe in. That is the kind of forgiveness I preach. It is a transaction within the human spirit.

I was once a farm boy. I learned that when it came time for eggs to hatch, we did well not to help the process along. The chick that had been helped in its birth could be spotted every time. It was weak, and it walked with a stagger. But that is what we do with the penitents who want to get right with God. Well-meaning people kneel down with the seeking sinners, find a Bible text and pray away until they see a little sign of life. Then, like eager midwives in the hen house, they pull the penitents from their shells, dry them off, write down their names as converts—and later wonder why they do not develop. But when the Holy Spirit brings penitents to the new birth, they bounce out into the world healthy and howling. Their sins are forgiven; their burdens have been lifted!

An observation

I close this chapter with just one other observation. It can be fatal to silence the inner Voice, the Voice of human conscience. Some silence it, for instance, when that Voice speaks in outraged protest at the human habit of lying. It may plead eloquently against the habit of dishonesty, or take a person to task for jealousy or for some other sin.

It is always perilous to resist conscience, to ignore the inner Voice. Let the Lord talk to your inner spirit, to your innermost being. Within you is a conscience that cannot lean on anybody, that cannot share the blame with anybody—a conscience that singles you out, isolates you and says, "You are the man!" "You are the woman!" It is the Voice that makes you want to lower your head and tiptoe away while no one is watching.

I am grateful for the human conscience. If there was no conscience and no voice of God in the world, we would all become beasts in very short order. We would all degenerate morally. In hell, where that Voice is not and where the conscience no longer exists, it is written, "He that is unjust, let him be unjust still: and he which is filthy, let him be filthy still" (Revelation 22:11). If that Voice is speaking to you—that inner Preacher who does not preach to a crowd but only to the lone individual soul—respond!

"Ye Are of Your Father the Devil"

We live in a day when it is very hard to find a genuinely sincere person. Most people are so caught up in the kind of society we live in that they are always pretending, always "putting on a front." They are never their real selves until they get mad, and when they get very mad, they begin to act naturally. They let go. It is sad and rather pitiful that about the only time you can find an American who is not a phony is when he or she is mad.

There was no pretense, no staging for dramatic effect, no make-believe in the encounter between Jesus and His declared enemies recorded in John 8. Jesus squarely confronted these Pharisees and other leaders who wanted to kill Him:

> Ye are of your father the devil, and the lusts
> of your father ye will do. He was a murderer

> from the beginning, and abode not in the truth, because there is no truth in him. When he speaketh a lie, he speaketh of his own: for he is a liar, and the father of it. And because I tell you the truth, ye believe me not. Which of you convinceth me of sin? And if I say the truth, why do ye not believe me? He that is of God heareth God's words: ye therefore hear them not, because ye are not of God. (John 8:44-47)

The atmosphere was that of the battlefield. We can almost hear the whistle of the artillery, the hostility and animosity and bitterness. We hear the firm, steady, severe words of Jesus, and we hear the angry, vehement, insulting attacks of those who were His foes. These men were mad, they were letting go, they had given up pretense. They were acting naturally, showing what they were within.

This was not theatrics just for show. It was a real battle, and real battles never take place in playhouses. This was warfare, and behind it were unseen forces. There were dark, sinister spirits animating those who had committed the unpardonable sin of opposing the Holy Spirit who was answering through the mouth of Jesus. Everyone was deadly earnest. These were spirits in conflict! Life and death were in that scene—and destiny and eternity! Heaven and hell were there, reflected in the force of the words exchanged between Jesus Christ and these vicious men.

A holy message

Actually, what our Lord had to say to them was holy, and it came from a holy heart. It came from a heart that later was to die for the very persons to whom He was speaking. Yet, because of the serious nature of their unbelief, our Lord had to impale them on the end of His spear. He turned them around so all the ages could see them.

There are always some who will argue that Jesus should have compromised, that He should have tried to get along with the Pharisees and Jewish leaders. We humans ought to notice something very wonderful and very different about the Lord Jesus. He was genuinely what He was, and He was never anything else but what He was. We presume that He could have got along with these folks better than He did if He had wanted to. He did not have to rub salt into the wounds, but He did. He did not lose His temper, but He never backed off.

Neither did He ever say anything that He later had to take back. You will notice that our Lord never had to apologize. He always said exactly what He meant and always with exactly the right amount of rebuke or love or compassion. If it had been His ministry to do it, He could have compromised and got on better. But He drew the line sharply and said, "He that is not with me is against me" (Matthew 12:30). He left no area open as a twilight zone. In the kingdom of God there will be no darkness, and in hell there will be no light. Jesus drew the line sharply between the darkness of hell and the light of heaven. He did not try to blend them into a compromising twilight.

In our day, churches are trying to offer such a compromise between heaven and hell. Some pastors feel this is the way to get along with people and to improve the church's public relations. Honestly, our Lord would have flunked any such test on public relations. People would not have given Him a grade of 30 percent. He would have flunked the whole thing because He was dealing completely in the area of truth, and truth is just truth—it never has to worry about its image. Truth never worries about the effect it will have, about who is going to hate it or who is going to accept it. It never worries about what there is to lose and what there is to gain.

Jesus is truth incarnate

Our Lord was truth incarnate, and that explains all of the conflict, all of the animosity. Perhaps He could have backed off and said the same thing in a gentle, half-hearted way. Then there would have been no line drawn. If He had done that, He would have pleased those who preferred to see heaven and hell join arms and go down the street in fellowship saying, "If we cannot agree, at least let's not disagree."

I think it is a different matter when we are concerned only with opinions—things that are not spiritual and issues that are not moral. If it is only a matter of taste, the decent thing to do is to say, "If we don't agree, let's not let it come between us!" But when the issue is a matter of spiritual conviction, the man who apologizes is a coward. In the case of Jesus and His enemies, they were not dealing with taste or etiquette, charm or art. They were dealing with eternal and spiritual issues. So Jesus had to tell them plainly, "Ye are of your father the devil" (John 8:44).

The Pharisees said, "Thou bearest record of thyself; thy record is not true" (8:13). Jesus responded, "Ye neither know me, nor my Father: if ye had known me, ye should have known my Father also" (8:19).

The Pharisees said, "Abraham is our father." Jesus responded, "If ye were Abraham's children, ye would do the works of Abraham" (8:39).

Jesus took every word they said, turned it around and, with calm severity, impaled them. He drove the spear straight through them. He held them up and turned them for the ages to see.

Some would still ask, "Why did Jesus do this?" Well, these people to whom He spoke were moral frauds. On the surface, their profession of religion was airtight. Probably there has never been any group anywhere who held a religious profession that was so tamper-proof. Look at them. Abraham was their father. They could trace the family tree right down to its roots. The genealogical tablets that meant so much to the Jews were destroyed when Titus took Jerusalem, but up to that time, these people could check the tablets for their tribe and their ancestry. They knew right were they belonged.

Then, of course, they had the temple and the holy place and the scroll of the Law. They had the carefully interlocking priestly service, and they all knew they were of God. They knew that; they were able to prove it. Their profession was impeccable.

The Light revealed the flaws

But now the Light of God was shining on them. This Light that lights every person was shining directly through their careful pretence, through their profession, through their fathers, through their synagogues, through their claims and their covenants.

Jesus frankly and simply faced them with three statements. Anyone who has ever studied basic logic will recognize the sequence: major premise, minor premise, conclusion.

Jesus said to them: "He that is of God heareth God's words." He reminded them, "Ye therefore hear them not." That left only one conclusion: "Ye are not of God" (8:47).

The major premise was one the Pharisees and Jewish leaders would readily accept: "He that is of God heareth God's words" (8:47). But they were then faced with the issue that in truth they were rejecting God's words. This is not sound logic; it is an accurate test of any man or woman in terms of whether or not he or she is of God. Is he, is she willing to hear the Word of God?

I should point out that to hear God's Word in the biblical sense of the term rarely if ever means to hear it the way you might hear a concert. Thousands of people listen to fine music regularly, but they just listen, they just hear it. It has no *moral* effect on them. They enjoy listening to good music, but the hearing leaves them neither better nor worse. But to hear the Word of God means to hear with sympathy, to heed and to obey. The person who is of God hears God's Word with sympathy. He or she heeds it, gives attention to it and obeys it. He or she does what the Word of God commands. If a person does not do these things, it is plain that he or she is not of God. If the men to whom Jesus spoke so severely had been truly of God, they would have heard and obeyed the truth. They would have been doing what was right. They would have kept the truth. But they did not!

That makes it easy for us to lay down an axiom to consider: We humans "do what we are." It is a statement that cannot be refuted. In other words, if we let ourselves go, giving up all outward pretensions, and live just from the desires within us, what we really are will come out. Basically, what we are is revealed by what we do, and what we do reveals what we are within.

What we are within is what counts

It is a plain truth, and it is really what our Lord was saying. What we are is more important than what we do. What we do is only a symptom of what we are. Consider, for example, the matter of temper. We are always finding a new stratagem to cover up that devil—temper! You never read anywhere that a man lost his temper. Instead, he "got upset." You never read that a woman lost her temper. Instead, she "had a case of nerves." But those expressions usually mean the person lost his or her temper—

"flew off the handle," "got mad." It is a spiritual, heart condition, not a nerve condition.

When people smile and nod their heads as I preach, that is not the real them. Those are more than likely conditioned reflexes. But when the same people have a temper upset, that is the real them. What they do out of their inner beings, out of their appetites, out of the explosions of their natures— that is really what they are.

Those human natures were exploding all around Jesus like bombs. Jesus told the Pharisees and other Jews, in effect, "All of these explosions of hatred and malice just prove what you are. If you were of God, you would not be doing this. You would be hearing and doing the Word of God. But you are doing what you are, and what you are doing *proves* what you are!

At this point we have to ask, "If this has been true all through the centuries, have there not been attempts to change human nature and human society?" Yes, mankind has been trying many ways to do something better with human nature. For instance, we try to do it by education. I believe in education. And I believe in training. Education is calculated to make us better citizens. Training conditions our reflexes so that we will behave in a predetermined pattern. But neither education nor training can provide us with new natures.

The bull out there in the farmyard is a domesticated animal, but once in a while he goes berserk. Unexpectedly, something will make him mad and he will explode. He will lower his head and roar and bellow. Anyone unfortunate enough to be in the field when that happens may have to climb a tree or jump over a bull-proof fence to keep from getting mauled! What has happened? That bull has simply risen in his anger and thrown off centuries of domestication. Underneath the domestication, he is really the same old wild beast, his nature unchanged.

Human nature is unpredictable

Once the bull is over his tantrum, he probably will be ashamed of himself and meekly follow his owner back to the barnyard. But the farmer does not know when the bull will go on another rampage, for he is dealing with a bull—an animal tamed through a long process of conditioning, but by nature wild.

And we humans are not much different. I read of a man with six years of graduate and professional training beyond college. But one day he blew up, lost his temper and killed his wife. Do not ever think that it is only the poor, the uneducated and the underprivileged who commit crimes of violence. It is happening in the top brackets of society, too. It takes more than education to change people's nature. Education may bring about certain restraints and some degree of control, but just let those people act freely from within, and you will find out what they really are.

Society has another way of trying to change people. That is by law. I am for law, too. But take, for instance, the trait of avarice. Avarice means the itchy hand, the love of money, and it is present in most people. If people are avaricious, nothing in the world is going to take that out of them. There is no cleansing water in the Ganges or any other river that will wash away their greedy bent. Not all of the soap in the supermarkets can avail to remove their avarice.

Lawmakers know that if avaricious people are turned loose in society, they may break and enter, or they may steal in other ways. So the lawmakers change avarice to larceny. In effect, they are saying, "If you express this avarice of yours, it is larceny." Therefore, people restrain themselves as best they can because they have been conditioned by society not to express the avarice that is within them. Often we do not even suspect these people because they have been placed under the restraint of law. But the avarice is still there, nevertheless. They are still avaricious people. They have avarice in their hearts. They hide it and restrain it because as soon as it comes out and is expressed, it changes color. It becomes larceny and the law will put them in jail.

Hatred is another example

Or, consider another example: hatred. There is no law against hate—as long as the hate is inside a person. Hate could never be proved in a court of law. It would do no good for lawmakers to decree that people could be fined or jailed for hating someone. The defendant could be as full of hate as Satan himself, but if he or she smiled pleasantly in the witness stand, the jury would bring in a verdict of "Not guilty!"

No, there is no law effective against hatred. So the lawmakers pass laws to prevent people from *expressing* hatred. Those who express it—by assault and battery, by manslaughter, by murder—are punished. These penalties are to keep the hatred inside people from coming out. We use education and our laws to damp the fires a little, but the old Adamic nature is still there.

Back to the confrontation between Jesus and the Jewish leaders, Jesus was saying to His foes, "See that smoke? The old sin-fires are still burning. Education and law have domesticated you, but you are like your father, the devil. You have murder in your hearts; you want to kill me." And Jesus proved that He was right, for they soon did kill Him.

Deal very much with the human race, and you will find that we are the sum of our consenting thoughts. Our Lord Jesus Christ gave us an illustration of that. Jesus was not only a teacher and a theologian, but He was a great philosopher. He knew why things were truth. When He quoted the Scriptures, He said why it was like it is. That is the only valid kind of Bible teaching, in my opinion.

Jesus said, "That whosoever looketh on a woman to lust after her hath committed adultery with her already in his heart" (Matthew 5:28). Consenting by thinking. If you think of the act with consent, you have done it, and if you have done it, you have done what you are.

When Jesus said to the accusers of the woman caught in the act of adultery, "He that is without sin among you, let him first cast a stone at her" (John 8:7), every one of those men looked within himself. Every one remembered his own consenting thoughts. Each looked at his own guilt, and man by man each of them sneaked away. They well knew there was not one among them who was worthy to throw a stone at the woman. According to the law of Moses, the woman should have died if her accusers were holy men, but there was not one there who dared to pick up a stone, and Jesus knew it. They all slunk away, red-faced and chagrined.

People are what they admire

That is an illustration of consenting thinking. Every person is really what he or she secretly admires. If I can learn what you admire, I will know what you are, for people are what they think about when they are free to think about what they will.

Now there are times when we are forced to think about things that we do not care to think about at all. All of us have to think about income taxes, but income taxes are not what we want to think about. The law makes us think about them every April. You may find me humped over Form 1040, just like everyone else, but that is not the real me. It is really the man with the tall hat and the spangled stars in Washington who says, "You can't let it go any longer!" I assure you it is not consentingly done! But if you can find what I think about when I am free to think about whatever I will, you will find the real me. That is true of every one of us.

Your baptism and your confirmation and your name on the church roll and the big Bible you carry—these are not the things that are important to God. You can train a chimpanzee to carry a Bible. Every one of us is the sum of what we secretly admire, what we think about and what we would like to do most if we became free to do what we wanted to do.

Consider the businessman working hard at his job. He may dream about doing something else, but circumstances force him to stay in that position. His wife has something to say about it. He is on that job, but within himself he is dreaming about what he would do if he were free to do it.

There is no doubt but that many men have been tamed like domestic animals. Many a husband has learned to say, "Yes, dear. Yes, dear." But when his wife is not there, you should hear what he says to the goldfish! At times he goes down the street bitter with anger, bitter with hatred, but he hides it at home because he has been trained by his wife.

Is there no hope?

The meekness and the obedience is not really him. What he thinks when he is alone—that is him. How he inwardly feels about things—that is him. Yes, we really are whatever we think about, whatever our instinct and our impulses are. Education and the law are not enough to transform our nature. Many a person has cried out in desperation, "Is there no hope? Is there no way that I can become something else? Is there no way that my human nature can be changed for the better?"

Perhaps you are reasoning deep within your own being. And you are ready to admit: "Mr. Tozer, you have been tearing at my heart. I know these things are true. I admit the logic of all this, and I know that I cannot stand clean before God. I know what I have done, I know what I think about, I know about the things I admire most—and it all indicates that I am not good. I ask you, Mr. Tozer, is there a way for me to become something other than what I am? Because I have hate in my heart, am I doomed to hell where hate must go?"

Thank God, there is hope! There is another way, for Jesus Christ offers us help. His Word tells us that we can get a new set of instincts, a new set of desires, a new set of appetites.

The help He promises is not based on our religious conditioning. The Lord Jesus is not speaking of applied religious psychology. He is actually speaking of and promising an entirely new biological deposit. He is promising something entirely new within our human spirit, so that when we do what we want to do we will want to do the right thing. The blessed truth is this: The person who wants to do the right thing and does it because he or she wants to do it is a good person!

The Savior, Jesus Christ, offers the remedy. He says there is hope for the avaricious person. God can take the avarice out and make that one generous to a fault. He says there is hope for the person of hot temper. God can cast the devil out of that temper and turn it in a holy direction.

There is hope for the jealous person. God can remove that jealousy and put in its place a zeal for the Most High God. God can give every one of us a whole new set of instincts, a new set of moral desires, a new moral bent so that we will do right because we *are* right. This is what the Word of God says. This is what the gospel promises. This is the call of Jesus Christ to those who are ready to follow Him and be His true disciples.

The gospel is more than a formula

Too often we have reduced the gospel invitation to a formula. "Put a nickel in the slot, pull down the lever, pick up your prize and go on your way. You believe on Jesus? Then take this tract and everything will be fine!" That may be the beginning of Christianity. It is something, but it certainly is not the sum of the gospel.

What does the Bible say about true Christianity? It says that if you will take Christ, follow Him and do what you should about Him, letting Him do what He wants with you, He will certainly take the bitterness out and put His love in. He will take the avarice out and put generosity in. He will take the hatred out and put peace in its place. That is what Christianity teaches and promises.

Those enemies of Jesus were perfectly sure that they were right because they believed the right things. They could have joined some of our fundamentalist churches that ask: "Do you believe the Bible? Do you believe it is God's inspired Word?" The Pharisees claimed to believe the right things. They appeared to be relatively right and clean. But there was hatred in their hearts.

We are what we do. And if what we do proves us to be wrong, then it is either live in despair or obtain the help we need. Thankfully, no one has to settle for despair. There is help.

Jesus Christ came to help. He came to change our natures. He came to stop old habits of sin. He came to break them and to conquer them.

You say, "I have received Christ. I believe in the gospel. I believe I am justified by faith. I believe I have peace with God through Jesus Christ, my Lord." You can say all of those things, but did you ever stop to think that all of that is bookkeeping? It is just religious bookkeeping.

I say, "I believe that I am justified. Nothing can separate me from God." That is bookkeeping. How do you know that means you? Has there been any change in your life, your desires, your instincts? You can claim all of this, but if you are not doing right and living right and being right and thinking right and wanting the right, you are *not* right!

Has there been any change? Is there a great difference since you came to Christ? Do you have that new nature so that you are a new person, a different person from what you once were? Jesus wants to make you what you ought to be. He wants to make you new and different. He wants to make you different on the inside—to give you a mind that runs clean and wholesome, no longer in the old channels.

He awaits your willingness to let Him take complete control of your life.

Being an Effective Witness for Christ

We are going to consider what it means to be an effective Christian witness as we look in John 4 at the encounter of our Lord with the Samaritan woman at Jacob's well.

There is a large amount of ineffective Christian testimony among us today. Much of it is well-intended, I am sure—honest and sincere. We do the best we can with what we have. But our performance turns out to be something like that of the salesman promoting fountain pens. He tries to make a case for his product, but his would-be customers know he really thinks ballpoints are far more practical.

Too much of our Christian witnessing is unconvincing because *we* have not been convinced. We are ineffectual because we have not yet capitulated to the Lord from glory. It is like the proselyte making proselytes.

I do not like to admit it, but for the most part Christians seem to be a very sad people. They are not the happy sort that they ought to be, and that is why their testimony is wavering and ineffective. The gleam has gone from their eyes and the shine from their countenances. Their testimony is no longer sparkling and contagious.

Perhaps this is happening because we are trying to plan how everything should happen. Everyone of us reads a little how-to book on witnessing. We try to do it the way we have been taught. But it is perfunctory and without any contagious element. If angels can weep, they must weep salty tears upon seeing a proselyte who has never really met the Lord making another proselyte who will also never meet the Lord.

The woman of Samaria met our Lord at the well. The Gospel account of what took place within her soul and the spontaneous, contagious witness that followed is rich with spiritual lessons for every one of us.

It is interesting to trace in the scriptural account how Jesus quickly drew the woman into a conversation about worship. Just as quickly, the woman told Jesus her belief that when Messiah came He would tell her everything.

Jesus announces His identity

"I that speak unto thee am he" (John 4:26), Jesus said to the woman. She had come from the city of

Samaria with her waterpot on her head. She had held a conversation with the most unusual man she had ever met—a Jew who had asked her for a drink. Now she was running back into the city, leaving her waterpot, to spread the word: "Come, see a man, which told me all things that ever I did: is not this the Christ?" (John 4:29).

We want to discover, if we can, why our Lord chose to disclose the great and holy secret of His Messiahship to a Samaritan woman. Why was He willing to reveal so much more about Himself in this setting than He did in other encounters during His earthly ministry? He talked about the meaning of His person, His life and His ministry to a woman—and to one who had not been a very good woman at that.

Why should this be? Around Jerusalem were plenty of priests with all of the proper credentials dating back to the very order of Aaron. There were many scribes—men appointed to make copies of the Scriptures and teach their meaning. There were lawyers skilled in the Mosaic law. There were religionists in numbers, for Israel was a very religious nation. If you and I had been doing it, we would never have chosen this woman with a shadow lying across her life as the receptacle for a holy secret. She was about to receive a divine revelation above anything that had yet been made and equal to anything ever to be made until after Christ's resurrection.

I do not know all of the Savior's reasons for choosing the woman at the well. I know that His revelation of Himself to her constituted an everlasting rebuke to human self-righteousness. I know that every smug woman who walks down the street in pride and status ought to be ashamed of herself. I know that every self-righteous man who looks into his mirror each morning to shave what he believes to be an honest face ought to be ashamed of himself.

Priests in their order, rabbis in their proper place, scribes at their tables and lawyers at their work were passed over, and this woman was given the holy secret. It was the secret of Jesus' Messiahship, the secret of the nature of God and the secret of the true nature of divine worship!

Jesus saw the potential

Jesus was able to see potential in the woman at the well that we could never have sensed. What a gracious thing for us that Jesus Christ never thinks about what we have been! He always thinks about what we are going to be. You and I are slaves to time and space and records and reputations and publicity and the past—all that we call the case history. Jesus Christ cares absolutely nothing about anyone's moral case history. He forgives it and starts from there as though the person had been born one minute before.

The woman with whom Jesus talked had led the kind of life that made her familiar with the men of Samaria. Likely she was much more familiar with the men of Samaria than with the women. Yet our Lord did not shame her, and He did not denounce her. Christians have quite a reputation for being among the great denouncers. The odd thing about it is this: they often denounce the ones whom the Lord receives with open arms and receive the ones the Lord denounces! That is how some carnal rascals get into our churches.

That is the danger of proselytes making more proselytes. It is possible for people to have some kind of an external religious experience that immunizes them to the new birth. Because they think they are already born again, it puts them where they will never be born again. The proselytes never were "in"; therefore, they do not require their proselytes to get "in," either. So it is possible that entire churches are comprised only of proselytes, echoes of echoes and reflections of reflections—never the true light shining.

It should be a profitable exercise to think back upon some of the reasons for Jesus' revelation to this woman at the well. There were a number of things that were in her favor.

One was her *conscious need*. There are some things that do not always follow—they are not always the same, and they lack in uniformity. But there is always uniformity in this area: every person who ever receives anything from God must have a conscious need, a conscious and vital sense of lack.

The Samaritan woman realized her need. She never fought back, for she was in great need, and she was completely frank about it. No doubt she had heard much religious argument in Samaria, and she was a good side-stepper. She did what she could to take the heat off as the Lord's kindly eyes bore into her conscience. But when she saw there was no use, she threw up her hands and was completely frank about her life and problems.

Her frankness impressed Jesus

The woman's frankness, humility and enthusiasm appealed to the Lord Jesus as they talked of mankind's need and the true worship of God by the Spirit of God. Jesus was drawn by her warm enthusiasm and by her frankness and her self-conscious need. So He revealed Himself, opening His own being to her, giving her the secret He had not given to anyone else and that He gave to very few in the days that followed.

When the woman spoke of the Messiah and His coming, and Jesus responded, "I . . . am he" (John 4:26), the revelation came to her own soul. The light of God slipped down into the shadows of her past and, there within her, it began to shine. She was so lifted in her being that she was compelled to run and tell her townspeople.

Jesus accepted the situation because He accepted the woman. I cannot see a church board anywhere that would have accepted such a woman. I think the women in their ladies' aid societies would have raised their eyebrows and made funny little clucking sounds with their tongues. But our Lord accepted the situation because He always begins as though there had not been a past. Behold, He makes all things new!

We can benefit, too, by noting the *fervency* and the *validity* of the woman's response. I would not deny that this woman still had a long way to go in her spiritual experience and development. But Jesus indicated God's willingness to use artless testimony and the sincere, candid witness, even though they may have been imperfect and limited.

The woman had this one gracious fact in her favor: she had had a valid encounter with the One called the Messiah. Her heart had come into collision with the revelation of the Person and the Will of God in Christ, and the result was an emotional upheaval in her own life and will.

Now, I confess that I do not know what to do with those Christian teachers who are afraid of *emotion*. Nowadays, we say that people are very emotional when we really mean they are neurotic, that they have lost self-control, that they cry over nothing, laugh over nothing, get blue over nothing, become elated over nothing. People like that are simply mental cases. We have taken the word *emotional* and applied it to that. But I disagree. That is not emotion. That is a mental condition, and those who have it need prayer and rest.

Emotion is inner feeling

When I use the word *emotion* here, I am referring to a person's inner feeling, and I am not afraid or ashamed to use the word in that way. I really prefer the expression used so often by Jonathan Edwards. He referred to our "religious affections." I wonder why someone does not resurrect that expression for our day. Jonathan Edwards could show some of our stiff, deep-freeze Christians that "religious affections" and the spiritual emotions of the modern day are one and the same thing. There are too many of us who go only on text and theology and are afraid of emotion.

So the Samaritan woman had come through a collision. Her heart had come into vital contact with the heart of Jesus Christ, and the result was a spiritual experience she would never forget. A stroke from God had fallen upon her, and it was little wonder that she started away without her waterpot. Probably she did not know why, but she was bursting inwardly to tell the good news that had come to her through the Messiah. It really was not much of a story at that time. The Lord knew that, but she did not. But it had about it the brightness of a revelation.

Notice this, too, about the sincerity of the woman's story and her actions: they were not imitative, they were not formal and, best of all, they were not programmed! I really hate that ugly French word *programmed*! We have to announce now that the service of worship is "programmed" so as to have a minimum of preaching and a maximum of enjoyment. But my point is this: If this woman could have been "programmed," there would never have been any revival in Samaria.

They did not program this woman. They could not. She had too much bounce in her soul! She was not involved in anything formal. She just went as fast as she could. No one planned her testimony for her (and thank God for that!). Sometimes I have been asked to meet with one group or another to "plan a revival." You might as well try to plan a lightning stroke as to plan a revival. No one has ever done it yet, and no one will ever really "plan" or "program" a true revival.

The Lord God Almighty makes a world, and nobody "plans" it. When He raises the dead, no one "plans" it. And—let me tell you this—when God raises the dead it never comes as the fifth item on the "program." Of that you can be sure!

Programmed into apathy

In our churches we have fairly well programmed ourselves into deadness and apathy. Think of this woman running to testify to the good news brimming over in her soul. If someone had halted her by grasping her garment as she ran and said, "Sister, we are glad to see the new light in your face and we would like to have you third on the program," she would have died along with those scribes and Samaritans and all the rest. But she went bouncing along, eager to share the new revelation which had come to her heart. She wanted to tell the men she knew that she had found the Master, the one who had told her everything she had ever done and known.

That was an exaggeration, of course. But, you know, when you get so full of something that you begin to talk about it, very often your mouth is smaller than your heart, and exaggeration is the result. We call it hyperbole now—that is the learned word for exaggeration.

This much must be said for the woman: she was *contagious*. She did not have to make converts. They caught the gospel from her!

Did you ever wonder about the result she produced with her breathless testimony? The men of Samaria heard her story and set out to find the Man about whom she had spoken. I suppose there was some curiosity involved, and perhaps an element of religious adventure, but certainly that was not all. These Samaritans, moved by this woman, went out and found Jesus and brought Him to the city. They saw Him and heard Him. They were convinced, and they believed. They testified, "Now we believe, not because of thy saying: for we have heard him ourselves, and know that this is indeed the Christ, the Saviour of the world" (John 4:42).

That which had begun in the shadows had now come into the clear sunlight. The testimony of the woman whose real life had only just begun brought these men to God. They found out the truth that you cannot rest on another person's testimony. You might just as well try to get fat on what someone else eats as to try to get to heaven on someone else's religious experience. A testimony itself does not convert you. This woman's testimony was used to bring people to Christ, but when they believed in Him, they said in effect, "Now we know for ourselves; we no longer need your testimony."

A Christian witness cannot save anyone

So this is the glory of the Christian witness. It serves to excite men and women and to get them going in the direction of the One about whom the testimony has been given. A Christian witness is not a spiritual experience for the other person. The witness itself never saved anyone. A Christian witness is an honest confession of what the Lord has done for us that may stir others to go and do likewise—to find the same Lord and His salvation.

I must confess that never in my whole life have I been blessed by a planned testimony service. In our church we have had many visiting musical groups. In the course of the concert a fellow says, "Now, we will give our testimonies." Everyone has been told ahead of time who is to talk and what he or she is to say. And I sit there just as cold as a dill pickle. I cannot find anything within me that responds to that kind of a witness.

But let me tell you the kind of testimony that really moves me. On a Sunday night about 11:30, my telephone rings. An excited voice on the other end of the line says, "Mr. Tozer, I had to call you and tell you something that couldn't wait until morning. I have been born again tonight! You know, I have been around your church with my wife, who is a Christian. She has been praying for me. Even though I thought I was a converted man, I have never been converted until tonight. After the service I came into a spiritual experience with Jesus and I *know* now that I am born again!"

I know that man to be a quiet fellow. I have no idea he can get so excited! He is pouring it on like an evangelist. He has a testimony. He has had an encounter with God. He is telling me what the Lord had done for Him. He is willing to admit that all of his previous religious experience has only been pre-liminary. Now he *knows*, and he can say to his wife, "Mary, now I know for myself!"

But if you try to plan a person's spiritual expres-sion and program his happiness, the testimony will start out dead and end up worse than dead.

A few conclusions

Now, let us draw a few conclusions from this account and apply them to our day.

First, *Christ is still receiving sinners*—even those who are great sinners. No matter what people's reputations may be, Jesus receives them if they will come to Him.

In Jesus' day, observers said with scorn, "This man receives sinners!" They were right. And He lived and died and rose again to prove it and to prove His right to justify all who come to Him in faith.

One of the old German devotional philosophers took the position that God loves to forgive big sins more than He does little sins because the bigger the sin, the more glory accrues to Him for His forgive-ness. I remember the writer went on to say that not only does God forgive great sins and enjoy doing it, but as soon as He has forgiven them, He forgets them and trusts the person just as if he or she had never sinned. I share his view that God not only for-gives great sins as readily as little ones, but once He has forgiven them He starts anew right there and never brings up the old sins again.

We have to be aware of the fact that man's forgiveness of man is not always like God's. When a man makes a mistake and has to be forgiven, the shadow may hang over him because it is hard for other people to forget. But when God forgives, He begins the new page right there, and then the devil runs up and says, "What about this person's past?" God replies: "What past? There is no past. We started out fresh when he came to Me and I forgave him!"

This kind of forgiveness and acceptance with God depends on a person's willingness to keep the top side of his or her soul open to God and the light from heaven. You may wonder about my expression, "the top side of the soul," but I do think it is in line with Bible teaching and certainly in line with all Christian experience. The top side of the soul is open to God in some people's lives and not in others.

At the risk of stirring some controversy over the implications of election and predestination, I refer you to the responses of two men in the Old Testament.

The examples of Jacob and Esau

Jacob was a crooked fellow. His very name meant "supplanter"—one who gains from another by treachery. He was not a pleasant man, and people did well to keep their wallets protected when he was around. But for some reason, he kept the top side of his soul open—there was a little window there that was open to God. Esau, his brother, had much more to commend him. He was less willful, he was more frank and outgoing, he was more tenderhearted (he wept on his brother's shoulder when he might have killed him). In every way, Esau was the finer man by nature. But in Esau there was no window open to God. It was Jacob, the crooked one, who met God and became Israel—"prince with God"—because the top side of his soul was open to God.

So it was with the woman of Samaria. She had not lived a moral life. But there was a vulnerable place in her soul, a window toward God that was open and through which the light of God could penetrate.

We should also know something else. *New life has to be born within us,* and that new life will not be born until there has been a collision with Christ. It must be a real collision. As sinners, our wills must be defeated at the cross. We must be brought down to the dust. It is an encounter we will always remember and look back up as happily we go forward in our faith. For a critical moment our souls and the heart of God met in violent conflict, but God won, and we surrendered, saying, "Thy will be done!"

This kind of spiritual encounter, this kind of meeting of the soul with God, comes as the freshness of a birth, a brightness of a dawning, the clearness of a revelation.

Let us not be guilty of taking our religion secondhand, of being "programmed" into our religion. We have been taught to accept what people tell us. As a result, we do not push on to know God for ourselves. A person who has to be picked out of the shell, who has to be guided by red lines and blue lines under the Bible verses and urged and pushed and psychologized into the kingdom of God never really gets in. There must be a revelation to the heart. There must be an encounter with Christ. There must be that sudden engaging of the soul with Jesus Christ, the Lord.

If our standards were higher, if we really proclaimed the truth of genuine repentance—does this sound like radical religion? It ought to be the normal, the ordinary thing. The Lord has told us that power must come to our lives. We must experience the presence, the revelation of God as we believe in Jesus Christ, His Son. This is not radical. It is the other thing—the deadness, the lack of power, the uncertainly—that is abnormal.

Thank God for every person who can say, "Yes, I met God and I know Him. We have had that collision. He won and I lost. And yet, I won because I am saved! My old will went down. My old boldness and aggressiveness went down. Jesus Christ came in and took over. Now I live no more, but He lives in me!"

If that has not been your experience, go to God with simplicity, frankness, hunger and conscious need. Go to Him as you are, without one plea, and the Lord Jesus will receive you and forgive you. You, too, can say, "I have heard this for years, but now I know for myself that Jesus is the Christ, the Son of the living God, the Savior of the world!"

The World Is a Moral Wilderness

The man sent from God whose name was John deserves a hearing. What he said about himself and about Jesus Christ is of vital and lasting importance. If we claim to be students of the prophetic Scriptures, we should take notice how John the Baptist answered those who came to check his testimony against their short list of possible identities:

> And he confessed, and denied not; but confessed, I am not the Christ. And they asked him, What then? Art thou Elias? And he saith, I am not. Art thou that prophet? And he answered, No. Then said they unto him, Who art thou? that we may give an answer to them that sent us. What sayest thou of thyself? He said, I am the voice of one crying in the wilderness, Make straight the way of the Lord, as said prophet Esaias. (John 1:20-23)

The "Jews of Jerusalem," who supposedly knew all the prophetic Scriptures, could not find a card for John the Baptist. It was not that the Scriptures had not foretold his coming. The Jews did not recognize him because they had put his card in the wrong file.

I do not want to distract you from the main flow of what I have to say, but let me stop to ask some questions about our own careful teaching of Bible prophecy. I wonder how many cards we have misfiled. How far have we missed God's plan? How many events may be on God's schedule about which we have done no thinking and no praying?

John's answers to their questions completely exhausted their list of expected people. They might as well have drawn it all out on a prophetic chart with crayon likenesses of the three prophets they were looking for. Then they could have intoned solemnly that they had God's last word on the subject.

John did not beat around the bush with these teachers. "I have been clearly foretold in your Scriptures," he said in effect. "Isaiah spoke of me, and you have overlooked his word. I do not fit into your plans because you want things your way. You want a dramatic prophet, a fiery Elijah. Of course you want the Christ, the King of Israel, to come. But on your terms. You have made no place in your expectations for someone who will disturb you morally. You want God to conform His intentions to *your* religious pattern, your religious tradition."

John was a new voice

When John came preaching in the wilderness, he attracted a wide following. There had been no prophet in Israel for 400 years. There had been no voice of God, no inspiration. There had been only the rabbis relating what others had seen and heard. These rabbis were the custodians of theology. Although they faithfully declared what others had heard from God, they themselves had neither seen God nor heard from Him.

These rabbis were disturbed when John came. As custodians of orthodoxy, they were disturbed by the appearance of a man who did not fit their mold. When they sent to inquire whether he was one of the expected ones, they betrayed the barrenness of their eschatological background.

If anything as sad as this can be amusing, it is almost amusing to consider how quickly these custodians of prophetic truth exhausted their list of expected ones. They asked, "Are you the Christ?" And John's answer was quick and blunt: "No."

"Well, then, are you Elijah?" Again John replied no. "Then are you the Prophet?" "No!"

Suddenly, there was John the Baptist, living out in the wilderness, getting unusual public attention. But he confessed that he was not the Christ, not the prophet Elijah, and not the Prophet. That is why the teachers told John that he did not fit, that they did not have a place for someone like him in their eschatological scheme. John challenged their traditions and their desire for the perpetuation of the status quo.

It was as if John said to them, "You want God to justify you. You want God to approve you and the narrowness of your vision. You cannot allow a prophet to come or a voice to be heard that will disturb you. You want to be left alone, but I have come to call you to righteousness. 'I am the voice of one crying in the wilderness, Make straight the way of the Lord' " (John 1:23).

Wilderness *was more than a place*

The word *wilderness* as John used it here does not have the same meaning it had when John was still in the wilderness before his manifestation to Israel. There *wilderness* meant an identifiable, discoverable piece of terrain that a person could mark on a map. But here, as is very often true in the Bible after a literal use of a word, there follows a figurative use of the same word. For an illustration, Jesus said to the Samaritan woman at the well, "Give me a drink." And then the conversation went from water to water. After the two had talked about the literal water in the well, Jesus said, "I will give you living water." He raised the woman's expectation from physical water to the spiritual.

John grew up in a literal wilderness, and now he says, "I am the voice of one crying in the wilderness." Obviously, this is a strong figure of speech, and its meaning is not confined to the wasteland where John had lived. It refers to the moral condition of Israel, for John was not talking about botany or zoology. He was talking about morality and religion. So he went from that time/space word *wilderness* straight to moral and spiritual considerations. The wilderness to which John addressed himself was the moral condition of Israel.

Consider some of the distressing characteristics of a wilderness. First, there is noticeable *disorder*. Go into a planned and maintained park and you will find order; go into a wilderness and you will find disorder.

Then there is *waste*. There may be great sections that are rocky, sandy, barren, without grass or growth save possibly for green briars, weeds and perhaps a scrubby tree here and there.

It is hard to find purpose in the wilderness. You can drive through parts of the Southwest and feel the desolation of the wilderness. I remember seeing in New Mexico a swayback old cow with noticeable ribs standing near the road. I wondered how she lived on the sparse grass and without enough water. There she was—just poor desiccated skin holding her bones together. In some wilderness areas of the West they jest that when God made the world, He had a big truckload of stuff left over and said, "Just dump it here!" It emphasizes the purposelessness, the lack of meaning in a true wilderness.

Then, there is the *wild*, undomesticated quality of the wilderness. Nobody seems to obey any law in the wilderness. The animals do not come when you whistle. They do not lie down and turn over when you speak. Because life in the wilderness is wild, there is confusion and disorder, waste and purposelessness. John had all of this in mind; he knew the wilderness and knew it well. He said, "That is what I see in Israel. God sent me to tell you what I see in Israel!"

It is happening here today

In our own generation here, there are attitudes and ways that godly men and women should be able to recognize for what they are. Maybe you think I am just getting old and there is a crack developing in the old dome. But I think I know what I am talking about. I am seeing something about the times and about the Christian church, and I hope there will be many others who see it, too, and rise up to do something about it.

John sensed and saw what the religious leaders of Israel could not perceive at all. He saw what the faithful custodians of orthodoxy never dreamed was true. They saw themselves in one light, and God saw them in another. John saw them the way God saw them. John and God were right, and the traditionalists were wrong. So John raised his voice for God and for truth in that wilderness.

It would be worthless to spend time here if we are simply to attack first-century Israel and vex our righteous souls with the conduct of long-dead Pharisees, scribes and Levites. But there is a present wilderness condition, a condition that parallels that of Israel in John's time. It amounts to this: even though we live in the world's most advanced civilization, we have been betrayed by our teachers—tragically and cruelly betrayed by our teachers!

Years ago our teachers told us that the world was getting better (I hesitate to use that worn-out cliche). They said, "Certainly the world is getting better." They cited the proofs. "We are able to cure rabies and control diabetes and other diseases. We are able to do so many things that we were never able to do before."

But there was a fallacy in their proposition. They supposed that because we had become brilliant toy makers, we had also become morally good toy makers. It is true that we have invented and developed and discovered all kinds of brilliant new toys. We can reach up into the skies, pull down the jagged lightning and put it in a box or run it along wires. We have learned how to transmit the human voice over great distances, at first only along wires, now without wires. We can send the human voice anywhere—even out into space.

A few generations ago toys were plain and simple. A boy would take a wheel and put a spike through it, split a stick and run the spike through the split stick, and he had a toy. A girl would take an old sock that was no longer useful, stuff it with cotton, paint a face on it, and she had a rag doll for her younger sister to play with. Now, such simplicity is left far behind. We live in a day of startling electronic and technological marvels. Artificial daylight instead of candles, supersonic transportation instead of oxcart. Instant communication worldwide instead of runner or pony express. And so our teachers have concluded that we must be better because we know so much more!

But one little thing has been overlooked in their preoccupation with our wonderful new ability to take the forces of nature and harness them. Our scientific and intellectual advances were not accompanied by similar moral strides. As our toy maker dreams came true, at the same time and in many of the same places, there came the most frightful and frightening, incredibly cruel and wicked state of affairs since the days of Noah. Gas chambers, pogroms, massacres, purges, mass starvation, concentration camps, brutalities, death marches—much of this utter disregard for human life has taken place in the very areas where our scientific advances were nurtured. Technology, instead of making us morally better, has been accompanied by a time of moral disintegration.

Do not quote me as saying that science has made us bad. But science *has not made us any better*—and something has made us worse. Attilla the Hun, Ghengis Khan, all of the cruel tyrants of the past—none could compare with these coldly scientific murderers of our own generation! And the wilderness characteristics have invaded other realms besides these.

I would like to say something about the degradation of women in our day. Probably there is no use, for no one believes it and to say it is like whistling into the wind. The degradation of women in all parts of the civilized world in this century has been winked at, excused and laughed off. But before the judgment bar of God it is not a laughing matter.

It is no more laughable than gangrene. If a man has gangrene in his leg and he can get enough people to glorify it and pay him to exhibit it and

write books and poems about it and sing songs
about it, he may be able to glorify gangrene. But
that will not change the nature of gangrene. It will
still kill him. Unless the doctors cut out that poi-
son and get all of it, it will kill him. You can never
come to terms with gangrene.

Spiritual gangrene

The illustration will stand in the spiritual realm.
When we violate the laws of God and bring pollution to the purest springs of the race, when we
build that moral pollution into our reasoning and
write books and plays about it and honor it, when
we continue to compromise on this issue and
then excuse and justify our compromising, we are
glorifying something that in time will kill us.

I am not sure we are going to see any change,
any repentance, any revulsion against this creep-
ing moral rot before judgment catches up with us.
I hope so, but I do not know. And I am not laying
all of the blame on the youth of our day. I am not
here to abuse the youth and their attitudes. Believe it or not, I was once young myself!

But there are frightening changes taking place all
around us. The rattiest little guy in the whole neighborhood just a few years ago would be common,
run-of-the-mill humanity today. Responsible gov-
ernment leaders and law officers and those of us in
parent-teacher associations and similar groups are
desperately worried because of the changing attitudes now held by segments of our youth. The
drugs that are coming into widespread use, the

quick marriages that are dissolving—and we know no better than to make jokes about such tragedies.

There has never been a time in history when people were good, but there have been times when the masses were ashamed of being bad. We have now degenerated to the point where we make belly-laughing jokes out of our evil ways and our scandalous morals. When the moral philosophy of a whole generation becomes such that people can flaunt their evil and rottenness and wind up being celebrated on the front pages of our newspapers, then God will withhold His hand no longer. We will rot from within. When we say this is the wilderness, we have our facts before us. The wilderness is all about us.

The church has been infected

If that is all we could see, I would say, "Thank God for a pure church in the midst of all this night! Thank God for a pure Bride of Christ shining forth His light in the midst of this present darkness!" But I cannot say that and tell the truth. The Christian church, instead of floating high above it all, free and clean and separated, finds her poor old boat leaking water from every seam. The church and the world have become so intertwined that it is hard to tell one from the other. The world has so affected the church's moral standards that Christians say they believe in Christ and yet have never bothered to change their moral attitudes and standards at all.

As in John's day, so it is in ours. The religious leaders were defending themselves and their traditions. They wanted to be left alone. They wanted to stand approved. They did not want to be disturbed. They wanted to go to church because "it is so peaceful there." They wanted to go to church so they could feel good. But all around them the wilderness conditions prevailed.

The cowardly leaders made converts, but it was to the morally purposeless and vain manners of the day. Now we preach the gospel, we say, and make converts—but we make converts to the wilderness, too! We make converts to the futility, the emptiness of a compromised church. I do not know if God will raise up another John the Baptist before the second advent of our Lord. If He should do so, one of the first things the church should get set for is to be disturbed—deeply disturbed. Perhaps even angered!

I assess the church of which I am pastor. Common honesty requires me to say that, compared with the average church, it is a good church. A large percentage of the members are good people and moral people. They could lead in prayer if called upon to do so. Many of them could help a seeking person find Christ. They contribute generously to missions and to other good causes. But even in my own congregation, how much disorder there is!

Compared with what the church ought to be, how much disorder there is in our lives—spiritual disorder in our lives and in our hearts! How much waste there is! There is waste of the vital gifts of God, waste of abilities of life and time. The wilderness is characterized by waste. And spaces that have gone to waste are no good to God or man.

You, perchance, may have to admit that the condition I have been describing describes your life, as well. Your heart may be more like a wilderness than like a garden, more like the stretches beyond Jordan than like the garden of God. Very little grows in the wilderness, and nothing really matures. If there is any fruit, it is scrubby. If there is any grain, it is inferior because of the barrenness.

I ask you, what will you have to show our Lord for your service? How tragic for a person to have been born again and yet to have no fruit to show for his or her Christian faith. How tragic to live life without having actually done anything for Christ!

The "Spiritual-or-Secular" Tightrope

In chapter 6 of John's gospel, the apostle records one of the two known instances when Jesus miraculously fed a multitude of people. Two disciples and an unnamed boy have roles in the Galilean drama: Philip, a man with a calculator; Andrew, a man with a suggestion; and a boy with a lunch he was willing to share. Look at the episode again:

> When Jesus then lifted up his eyes, and saw a great company come unto him, he saith unto Philip, Whence shall we buy bread, that these may eat? And this he said to prove him: for he himself knew what he would do. Philip answered him, Two hundred pennyworth of bread is not sufficient for them that every one of them may take a little. One of his disciples, Andrew, Simon Peter's brother,

saith unto him, There is a lad here, which hath five barley loaves, and two small fishes: but what are they among so many? And Jesus said, Make the men sit down. Now there was much grass in the place. So the men sat down, in number about five thousand. And Jesus took the loaves; and when he had given thanks, he distributed to the disciples, and the disciples to them that were set down; and likewise of the fishes as much as they would. (John 6:5-11)

Just prior to this miraculous multiplying of the bread and fish, Jesus "went up into a mountain, and there he sat with his disciples" (6:3). The fact is noteworthy. It seems plain that Jesus withdrew purposely from the great press of people who had been pursuing Him.

There are some things that you and I will never learn when others are present. I believe in church and I love the fellowship of the assembly. There is much we can learn when we come together on Sundays and sit among the saints. But there are certain things that you and I will never learn in the presence of other people.

Unquestionably, part of our failure today is religious activity that is not preceded by aloneness, by inactivity. I mean getting alone with God and waiting in silence and quietness until we are charged with God's Spirit. Then, when we act, our activity really amounts to something because we have been prepared by God for it.

Be sure it is the right inactivity!

Those among us who practice inactivity generally do not practice the kind of inactivity recom-
mended in the Bible—the kind of quiet waiting on
God that our Lord practiced. Some of what we see
today is just plain laziness, and the Lord has nothing good to say about the sluggard. There is not one
lonely text in the 66 books of the Bible that says anything kind about the sluggard. The inactivity that
arises out of sheer laziness has no place in the Bible.

There is also the inactivity that stems from fear.
People who are fearful of doing anything at all
figure they can narrow the area of their peril by
doing nothing. They think if they simply stand
still, there will be less danger of getting into trouble. God never sanctions this kind of inactivity,
for it springs from an unchristian motive.

Others are inactive because they lack vision. They
just do not know what to do, so they do nothing!
Great sections of the church are in that condition.
These are people who have never seen a path, and
they do not know where to find one. They have no
highway stretching ahead, so they stand still.

But there is an inactivity which, paradoxically,
is the highest possible activity. There can be a sus-
pension of the activity of the body, as when our
Lord told His disciples to "tarry ye in the city of Jerusalem, until ye be endued with power from on
high" (Luke 24:49). They waited. And the Holy
Spirit came on them in power.

In the Old Testament, to wait on God meant
coming before His presence with expectation and

waiting there with physical and mental inactivity. "Cease thy thinking, troubled Christian," one of the old poets wrote. There is a place where the mind quits trying to figure out its own way and throws itself wide open to God. And the shining glory of God comes down into the waiting life and imparts an activity.

Do you understand what I mean when I say that we can go to God with an activity that is inactive? We go to God with a heart that is not acting in the flesh or in the natural—trying to do something. We go to God in an attitude of waiting. It just means that our inner spirit is seeing and hearing and mounting up on wings while our outer, physical person is inactive and even the mind is to some degree suspended.

Jesus once rebuked a too-active woman

We know that Jesus once rebuked a woman for being too active. She was Martha of Bethany. Sometimes we are prone to add to what the Lord actually said to Martha. His kindly rebuke has been a cue for preachers to heap abuse upon the poor woman. I personally thank God for the Marthas in the world. Someone generally has to cook and do the dishes and see that the work gets done. Without Marthas, we would not be so sleek and well-fed. We should let the Lord's rebuke be sufficient without adding to Martha's chastening.

But notice on the other hand that Mary was there, simply sitting. It is the same word that John uses for the inactivity of Jesus when He went up into the mountain and sat with His disciples. Mary was simply sitting at the feet of the Savior, and the Lord rebuked Martha for her nervous activity. I think she just carried her activity beyond the point where it did any good, and she did not back it up by an inward spiritual relaxation.

Now, in the case of our Lord, the people came to Him, John reports, and He was ready for them. He had been quiet and silent. He had sat alone with His disciples and meditated. Looking upward, He waited until the whole hiatus of divine life moved down from the throne of God into His own soul. He was a violin tuned. He was a battery recharged. He was poised and prepared for the people when they came.

So the people came—a great mob of humanity that three days before had charged out of the surrounding Galilean towns to follow the Teacher. Some brought their babies, and some were elderly and not physically strong for this kind of trekking. Now, after three days on the way, their food had given out. They were in need, but there was no place where they could buy food.

It was then that the Lord asked Philip, "Whence shall we buy bread, that these may eat?" (John 6:5). Does that question say anything to you? It says to me that our human Lord was concerned about bread and people's natural hunger.

I know of no camp meeting ground without a kitchen and dining hall. There has never been a pentecost that did not have a cook somewhere around the corner to feed the Spirit-filled saints.

Our Lord knows that we are human beings. It is good for us to know that He understands us and our need for food.

Our bodies are a discipline

I have wondered why God gave us bodies and tied us down to them. I have concluded that He did so more or less as a discipline. I do not know what else they are for. Emerson wrote that nature had one function toward human beings, and that was to discipline them.

At least occasionally we are bound to think like this. The body at times gets a little out of hand, and we have to spend as much care and energy looking after it as we spend doing everything else we do. I am glad God understands about it. I am glad He knows. He gave us these mortal frames, and He expects us to take care of them. We see in this setting that He was concerned about the people having something to eat.

I have never believed in the great distinctions that some try to make between the sacred and the secular. Eating can be just as religious an act as praying. It is just as spiritual for me to eat my breakfast as it is to have family prayers. When we separate our breakfast from our prayers, we are making an unnecessary division. Why should we put eating in one category and apologize to the Lord, saying, "I'm awfully sorry, Lord, but You know I have to eat now. I'll see You as soon as I am through, but please excuse me now while I take time to eat."

It is wrong to place our physical necessities on one side and put praying and singing and giving and Bible reading and testifying on the other side. How can we say "This is spiritual" and "This is secular"? We actually try to walk a tightrope between the two, the secular and the spiritual, apologizing to God when we must turn aside for a little while to do something "secular."

Well, I have a better way than that for living, and I can tell you the Lord Jesus never made the distinction that many Christians do. He said He was the Lord. He was God Himself, and He asked, "Where shall we buy bread for these people to eat?" When He broke the loaves and passed them along to that great multitude, they ate, and the eating was as spiritual as the teaching of the preceding days had been. The teaching and the eating were equally spiritual, and the praying that preceded the meal was just as spiritual—but no more so—than the eating.

The Lord of our bread

If you can get hold of that, it will mean a wonderful thing to you. The Lord is the Lord of our bread, the Lord of our eating, the Lord of our bathing, the Lord of our sleeping, the Lord of our dressing, the Lord of our working. When we work we need not say, "I have to work today, but I'll plan to have some time with You this evening." Our Lord is with us, sanctifying everything we do—provided it is honest and good. If your job is decent and respectable, the Lord is going to bless it, and if the Lord is in you, He will be in your labor as well.

Notice that it was the Lord of Glory who said, "Whence shall we buy bread, that these may eat?" (John 6:5). He Himself was concerned with the people's need for food. But He made it Philip's problem. He honored Philip by letting him participate in the solution.

I once preached a sermon in which I said that the Lord is self-sufficient and does not really need us. I bothered some people by that, for they thought the Lord really needed them. They thought that if they should resign or retire, the Lord would have to scramble to find someone who could take their place. What a low view of God! Could you get down on your knees and cry out to a God who needed you? I could not. A God who needed me would be a God in real trouble. God does not have to have me—or you, either. That may be bitter medicine for some to take, because we have come to believe that we are indispensable and that, when we go, a great tree will have fallen, leaving a vacant place against the sky. I am afraid that when some of us die, it will be like a stalk of grass eaten by a grasshopper, and nobody will notice the difference!

But here were these hungry people, and the Lord was going to feed them. The thing is, He did not want just to feed them and have it over with. He wanted some blessing to flow all around as a result of it. So He picked out one of His disciples—Philip—saying to Himself, *I am going to bring Philip into this. I am going to honor him by letting him become a part of this plan. He can help Me work it out, although actually I do not need him at all.*

So Jesus encouraged Philip to tackle the problem along with Him. He nudged Philip a little and got him into a hard spot, just to reveal to Philip his own emptiness.

It is never a waste of time to learn that you do not know every answer, and it is never a waste of time to learn how little you have. It is a positive victory for me when I learn the things I cannot do—and the things that I do not have.

The Lord can fill what we empty

Actually, there is so little filling of our vessels these days because we do so little emptying of them. The Lord had to empty Philip in order that He might fill him, for Philip was full of his own ideas. The Lord cannot fill with His own presence that which is already full of something else. To be frank, Philip did not acquit himself very well when Jesus asked him where they would buy bread for the people to eat.

Philip revealed the type of mind that is altogether earthly, uninspired and uninspiring. He reached for his calculator, pressed the "on" switch, and went to work. I call him Philip the Calculator.

People are not nicknamed quite as much as they used to be. People used to be nicknamed for what they were. Even in rural western Pennsylvania when I was growing up, people were distinguished by their nicknames. And if you will look back in history, you will find men with distinguishing names, such as Eric the Red and Alexander the Great.

Here in the New Testament was Philip the Calculator—Philip the Mathematician, Philip the Clerk. There was need for a miracle, and Philip set out to calculate the odds. Probably every Christian group has at least one person with a calculator. I have sat on boards for many years, and rarely is there a board without a Philip the Calculator among its members. When you suggest something, out comes the calculator to prove that it cannot be done.

Before our Chicago church relocated, there was an old milk barn on the site. When we talked about building, we had plenty of Philips who said, "It can't be done!" And of course they could prove it. But we built the church anyhow and had the building paid for in six short years. But the Philipses said, "It can't be done," and they had the calculations to prove it.

As I say, I have been sitting on these boards for many years, and there are always two kinds of board members: those who can see the miracle and those who can only see their calculators and their strings of calculations. Philip went to work with his calculator. He knew how much money there was among the disciples. He knew how much a loaf of bread cost. He knew the size of the hungry crowd.

One hundred percent negative

Philip cranked all those statistics into his calculator and came up with his answer. "Eight months' wages would not buy enough bread for each one to have a bite!" Philip had made his contribution, and it was 100 percent negative. If Jesus and the other disciples had listened only to Philip, they and the multitude would have starved in the wilderness. The glorious miracle would not have taken place.

All you have to do to kill a church is to talk it down. Just let the sheep begin to bleat the blues, and the church will die in no time at all. The power of suggestion will likely care for the rest of the downfall. One fellow will meet another and say, "Things aren't going so well at church, are they?" "No, not so well," the other responds.

Another fellow comes up to man number two: "Things don't seem to be going very well at the church," he comments. "That's what I have been hearing," says man number two. He heard it just five minutes before from man number one. So it soon comes out: "Have you heard what the talk is? Things aren't going very well at the church." Before very long, they have talked that church down. The people with the calculators have seen the problem, but they have not seen God. They have figured things out, but they have not figured God in.

Philip the Calculator. He can be a dangerous man in the church of our Lord Jesus Christ. Every suggestion made in the direction of progress gets a negative vote from this man.

The man with the suggestion

Next we come to the other man, Andrew. Andrew did a little better than Philip. He made a timid suggestion: "There is a lad here, which hath five barley loaves, and two small fishes: but what are they among so many?" (John 6:9).

I would not call Andrew a world-beater on the basis of this account. If he were living today, he would not be known as a founder or a promoter—that is for sure. Andrew was only partly over on the side of the miracle. Andrew overheard Philip's answer and probably thought, *Surely Philip's final tally is off base. Philip is a good man and I like him, but he is a bit on the negative side.* Andrew looked at all the figures on Philip's printout: so much bread for so many pennies; so many hungry people; break each loaf into so many pieces—*No,* Andrew thought, *it is no use. Philip is right: There would be merely a trifle for each person, even if we had the money. But this can't be the end. There must be an answer. There must be a way.*

So Andrew began to look around. You will be getting a little closer to the miracle when you can get a church full of Andrews. Even if you have only one or two of them, you will usually hear one of them say, "There is a boy here with a lunch, some bread and fish, but then, after all, that's not very much—" And there is a rising inflection in his voice, which is an invitation for someone to come to his rescue. "If I can get an encouraging word from someone, I think I can see some hope in this situation." That is Andrew.

You are getting a little warmer when you are like Andrew! Philip was as cold as ice, with his calculator and his proof that no one was going to eat on that occasion. Andrew looked around and said,

"Well, we have a start. We have a little lunch here. A little basket. A boy."

I have never been able to figure out how that boy managed to hang onto that lunch. Boys whom I know would have had it eaten by nine o'clock the first morning, and here it was the third day! But he was still holding onto the little lunch. Perhaps his mother had given him some extra food and he still had it. The five loaves were really only pancakes in size and shape. That is all they were—plus two small fish.

So that was the boy. Andrew himself had nothing, but he knew that a boy had a little lunch. The lunch might help out a bit. I think of Andrew as being a help on any church board. At least he was looking around for a fellow with a lunch. This speaks of hopefulness, of at least a little faith.

We need some Andrews

It is time we find an Andrew or two—people who have hope and faith to look around for at least a token of help. That is all that lunch was: merely a token. It was not very much. It really was not enough for more than one. But Christ took that inadequate token and made it enough for more than 5,000 people.

Sometimes I have quoted a little passage I got from dear old Walter Hilton, who lived before the time of Shakespeare. He was talking about serving God and how we ought to go about it. He said, "I will give you a little rule." Then he used the Old English word *mickle,* meaning much. "Mickle have, mickle do. Let have, let do. Nothing have, at least have a good intention." *If you have much, do much. If you haven't much, do what you can. If you haven't anything, have good intentions.* That is a good rule. Andrew at least had good intentions. He found a lunch—a token. He was on God's side.

You may have noticed that John does not really tell us how they got that lunch. He says that Jesus took the loaves; he does not say how He got them. But I have read too much about my Lord to believe that there was any coercion involved. That lunch must have been vitally important to the boy, but he surrendered it to Jesus.

Perhaps Jesus smiled and said to the boy, "Would you like to do something that would help all of these hungry people?" And the happy-faced boy replied, "Certainly, Master."

"Then, may I have your lunch?" I think the boy grinned and handed it over to Jesus, who turned to His disciples and said, "Have the people sit down." So they sat down in orderly rows, in tiers of rows, and Jesus took the bread and blessed it, lifting up His heart and saying, "O God, bless this little bit. Bless this little bit of optimistic hope. Bless this token of belief."

And then Jesus began to spread around the barley bread and the fish, and suddenly there were baskets full. Where did the baskets come from? They were the lunch baskets from which the people had eaten a day or two before. There had been plenty of empty baskets in that crowd, but only one lunch. Jesus took the one lunch and multiplied it so there was food for all. Because it had been surrendered for His use, it became the blessing of more than 5,000 people.

Some personal questions

All of this brings us to some personal questions. Are you a Philip? an Andrew? a boy with a lunch?

Philip was so good at calculations that he forgot to figure God into the equation. Andrew was a little nearer. He did not have anything himself, but he knew where he could dig up something. And then there was the boy. He did not have much, either, but what he had he gave to Jesus, who had the power to make it sufficient.

Which side are you on? Are you with those who are convinced that the Lord cannot do anything in this situation? Do you have out your calculator to prove the situation's impossibility?

Are you among the uncertain ones, whose hearts are on the right side? You are sure that the lunch is not enough, but you are hopeful because it is something.

Perhaps you are with the boy, who says, "If I give you this lunch, Master, it means I may not eat. But I like the way You do things, and I am willing to go along with You. You may take my lunch."

I might as well tell you right here what I think. I think when the Lord sent a basket of that food to the boy, He put an extra fish on top! It would be quite in keeping with the ways of the Lord—to put a little extra in the basket of the fellow who had given his all. I know He does this in spiritual things, so why should He not do it with a lunch?

I recommend that we ask God for at least the faith of an Andrew, and that we begin to look around for tokens of the grace of God. Surely we will find these tokens. You yourself may have a token and not know it. Do you think the boy knew that he had the key to the miracle? No, he did not know. But in fact he carried it in his lunch basket. He had lugged it for three days and did not know it.

You may have in your possession the key to the future. You may have in your hand, without knowing it, the key to the salvation of at least ten people, and perhaps a hundred, if you only knew it. You need only surrender that key to the Lord and let Him have it.

Say to Jesus now, "Master, I only have a token, a little token, but take it, Lord Jesus, take it!" The Lord will take it. How He will multiply it I do not know, but He can do it.

And He will.

The Church Is on a Stormy Sea

This final chapter is intended to be a message of encouragement in a time of political, social and economic upheaval. In the midst of all the turmoil on earth, there is One walking through the storm. His name is Jesus. He is Christ the Lord. We ought never be frightened—even for a moment—because Jesus is the Sovereign Lord.

The apostle John informs us that after Jesus had fed the multitude, our Lord perceived that the satisfied people "would come and take him by force, to make him a king." So Jesus "departed again into a mountain himself alone" (John 6:15). It is there that we pick up the narrative:

> And when even was now come, his disciples went down unto the sea, And entered into a ship, and went over the sea toward Capernaum. And it was now dark, and Je-

sus was not come to them. And the sea arose by reason of a great wind that blew. So when they had rowed about five and twenty or thirty furlongs, they see Jesus walking on the sea, and drawing nigh unto the ship: and they were afraid. But he saith unto them, It is I; be not afraid. Then they willingly received him into the ship: and immediately the ship was at the land whither they went. (John 6:16-21)

Note the elements of action. Jesus withdraws to the mountain, presumably for reflection and prayer; in the gathering evening darkness, the disciples set out by small ship for Capernaum, their home base. A sudden tempest turns Galilee into an angry sea, and the frightened disciples struggle in their storm-tossed boat. Then they see Jesus walking on the water. Assured that it is He, they take him into the ship, and, miraculously, they are at their destination.

This episode becomes a prophetic drama of the church as she awaits the return of her Lord and the predestined summation of all things. It was not by coincidence that our Lord went up into the mountain and the disciples went down to the sea. I believe the Lord was giving us a very beautiful object lesson, leading us into thoughts concerning the hope of His return to earth. With all my heart I believe that Jesus will return soon. I believe He will walk on our troubled sea, just as He walked on the Sea of Galilee to His struggling disciples. Perhaps we think we do not need Him badly enough. When our need here is so great that we can no longer get along without Him, He will come!

An inspiring Lord Jesus

There are some beautiful and inspiring things we should note about the Person of the Lord Jesus Christ as we proceed. As I have mentioned, after feeding the 5,000 people, Jesus perceived that the gratified, enthusiastic crowd wanted to take Him by force to make Him their King. So He departed again into a mountain alone, the disciples meanwhile going down to the sea to board a small ship that they would sail or row to Capernaum.

Notice first that Jesus declined the offer of the multitude to make Him King. The average man would not have declined a crown, but Jesus Christ is not the average man; He is the Sovereign Lord of the universe. He declined their offer of a crown because He knew the crown they wanted to give Him was not the crown He was destined to wear. Our Lord knew, also, that this was not the right time for a crown. He knew a cross awaited Him before there could be a crown.

We can be assured that our Lord Jesus Christ never did the expected thing, as other men might do. To my mind, He is the supreme Poet and Artist and Musician of all the world. All that is beautiful and lovely and gracious and desirable gather themselves up in our heavenly Bridegroom.

His birth was not a common birth, for our Lord stooped to mortal flesh to be born of the virgin Mary. He has, by the manner of His birth, elevated and dignified human birth beyond all possibilities of description.

The work Jesus did was not common work, even though He humbled Himself to work at the carpenter's bench. What He did was to elevate all labor to an uncommon level and to dignify the most humble toil.

Jesus suffered when He was on earth, and yet His suffering was not the common, tight-lipped, cold-eyed suffering that goes on in our world. It was not the suffering that destroys the higher regions of the spirit and bestializes us, making us like the clay from which we came. The suffering of our Lord was uncommon because everything He did and said rose infinitely above the level of the common.

Raised above the common level

If we belong to Jesus now in faith, He has raised us above the level of the common, so that we ourselves as children of God no longer do what is common. It is this elevation of things by the suffering Savior that explains why the most common act becomes an extraordinary act when it is done by the believer in the spirit of Christ's compassion.

Our Lord also stooped to die, but His dying was not the common dying of a man. It was not the discharge of a debt to nature. It was not the final payment on a mortgage held over Him by nature. Nature never held a mortgage on Jesus Christ. He was nature's Creator, not her debtor.

What made Jesus' death uncommon, unusual? It was the dying of the just for the unjust. It was His sacrificial dying, His vicarious dying. He paid a debt He did not owe in behalf of others too deeply in debt ever to pay out.

Being that kind of a Lord in His life and in His death, it is to be expected that His words were never common words. We understand well why His words never will be comprehended by rank-and-file, unconverted men and women. But we understand, too, why His words have always fallen like grace and truth upon the ears of the humble in heart and the meek in spirit.

Has this not been the testimony through the years of all the saints of God? They have come to the Scriptures like bees to flowers, carrying away the sweet and precious nectar for their spiritual needs. But then they have returned again and found that there was still as much nectar as there had been before. Like the Zarephath widow's barrel of meal that was not used up and the jug of oil that did not run dry (see 1 Kings 17:7-16), every text of Scripture, every word of our Sovereign Lord, yields precious treasures no matter how often we consult it, no matter how acute our need.

So it was with the acts of Jesus. We see it in our Lord's refusal of the crown and His withdrawal to the mountain. If Jesus had stooped to receive the crown they offered, Israel would have rallied behind Him in a moment. But Jesus took the cross in the will of God rather than a crown out of the will of God. What meaning, what direction there is for each of us here!

It takes some of us a long time to learn that the crown before the cross is only worthless tin. It is cheap and gilded, and when we examine it closely we see the inscription "Made in Hell." It is not a crown that came down from heavenly glory but a crown that came from below—a false crown for the person who will take it before he or she takes the cross.

The will of God is always best

At the risk of repeating a religious cliche, I must point out that the will of God is always best, whatever the circumstances. Jesus refused the crown and deliberately took the cross because the cross was in the will of God, both for Him and for humankind.

Let us not be afraid to take that cross ourselves and trust God to provide the crown in His own time. Why should so many in our day try to short-circuit their spiritual lives by eliminating the cross en route to the crown?

Our Lord took the Father's will. He refused the crown that Israel wanted to give Him and instead took the cross the Romans gave him. On the third day He arose from the dead. Forty days later, He ascended to His Father's right hand, His disciples seeing Him go. And there He is today!

Back to the episode in John 6, what did Jesus do when He was in the mountain alone? He prayed. Jesus, that praying Man of all praying men, that example of all praying men, was talking to His heavenly Father. He was talking to Him about the little group of disciples whom He had just parted from a short time before—and about the 5,000 people who had just been fed and in their ignorance wanted to make Him their King.

By the human reckoning of the multitude, Jesus would bring about a revolution that would set Israel free, as in the days of Gideon and the great judges and prophets of the Old Testament. But Jesus knew these people well. He knew the worst thing He could do would be to put on a crown and bring that carnal multitude into an earthly kingdom.

Actually, there would have to be many changes among them before they dared become sons and daughters of an earthly kingdom. So He was praying for them in their ignorance and in their confusion, praying to the heavenly Father for His sheep. *And that is exactly what He is doing now!* Jesus is in heaven, praying for His people. I do not mean that our Lord is on His knees continually in the glory land yonder, but He is in continual communion with the Father. "Wherefore he is able also to save them to the uttermost that come unto God by him, seeing he ever liveth to make intercession for them" (Hebrews 7:25).

Praying without ceasing

Years ago, dear old Max Reich, who spoke in our church a number of times, was asked to describe his prayer life. "If you are asking me about getting by myself and spending long periods alone on my knees in prayer, then I would have to say that I am relatively a prayerless man," Dr. Reich told us. "But if you accept praying without ceasing as a continual, humble communion with God, day and night, under all circumstances—the pouring out of my heart to God in continual, unbroken fellowship—then I can say I pray without ceasing."

I believe this is the manner in which our Lord is remembering us at the Father's throne. His communion with the Father speaks to us of the necessity of a continual communion of our souls with God. This kind of communion and devotion does not consist of words.

I once wrote an editorial which I titled "Wordless Worship." In it I tried to present the idea that there is a worship that goes beyond human words. In fact, I have come to the conclusion that whatever can be put into words is second rate, for there are divine spiritualities that cannot be expressed.

In fact, Paul called these divine spiritualities "inexpressible." They are the eternal things that do not pass away. It is here that we need to remember that God is allowing us to live at the same time on two planes. He permits us to live on the religious plane, where there are preachers and song leaders and choirs and organists and pianists and editors and leaders and promoters and evangelists. That is religion. That is religion in overalls—the external garb of religion. It has its place in God's work and plan. But beyond and superior to all of the externals in our religious experience is the spiritual essence of it all. And it is that spiritual essence for which I plead. I long to see it enthroned in our communion and fellowship in the church of Jesus Christ.

We have many Bible conferences that begin and end in themselves. They circle fully around themselves, and after the benediction everyone goes home no better than he or she was before. That is the woe and the terror of these conferences. I plead for something more than textualism that begins and ends with itself and sees nothing beyond.

We must press on in the Holy Spirit

If we do not see beyond the visible, if we cannot touch that which is intangible, if we cannot hear that which is inaudible, if we cannot know that which is beyond knowing, then I have serious doubts about the validity of our Christian experience. The Bible tells us

> Eye hath not seen, nor ear heard, neither have entered into the heart of man, the things which God hath prepared for them that love him. (1 Corinthians 2:9)

That is why Paul goes on to remind us that God has revealed these mysteries to us by the Holy Spirit. If we would only stop trying to make the Holy Spirit our servant and begin to live in Him as the fish lives in the sea, we would enter into the riches of glory about which we know nothing now.

Too many want the Holy Spirit in order that they may have the gift of healing. Others want Him for the gift of tongues. Still others seek Him so that their testimony may become effective. All of these things, I will grant, are a part of the total pattern of the New Testament. But it is impossible for us to make God our servant. Let us never pray that we may be filled with the Spirit of God for secondary purposes. God wants to fill us with His Spirit in order that we should know Him first of all and be absorbed in Him. We should enter into the fullness of the Spirit so that God's Son may be glorified in us.

I try to bathe my soul in the writings and the hymns of the devoted saints of God who lived centuries ago. These were men and women who walked with God, then were no more because God took them to Himself. They left behind such themes as "Jesus, Thou Joy of Loving Hearts" and "Jesus, the Very Thought of Thee with Sweetness Fills My Breast." When I sense the shining glory of the life and works of these choice saints of the past, I wonder why we ever stoop to read or sing or quote anything but that which is elevated and divine, noble and inspiring.

Jesus prays for us

Jesus declined the crown. Instead, He went up into the mountain. His presence there actually *is* prayer. At the Father's throne He is not everlastingly naming His people in pleadings and petitions. He is not talking on and on, as some of us do, covering our inward fears by our multitude of words. No, it is His presence at the right hand of the Father that constitutes His intercession for us. The fact that He is there is the might of His prayer, and that prayer is for His people—for you and me and for the whole church of Jesus Christ.

In this Galilean drama, it is not difficult to envision the Christian church. As it is told in the first two chapters of the Acts, Jesus had not more than reached the heavenly mountain when suddenly the disciples were filled with the Holy Spirit and the church of Christ was launched on the sea, on the dark sea. And she has been on that sea ever since.

When our Lord went up into the mountain and the clouds received Him out of their sight, the Light of the world went away, and night came. Jesus had warned His disciples, "Yet a little while is the light with you. Walk while ye have the light, lest darkness come upon you" (John 12:35).

It is altogether true that night has settled on the world, and the church has worked in darkness through the years. I do not mean that the church has had no light, but I do say that the condition of the world has been darkness, and it has been as night upon the world throughout these centuries. The Dark Ages in history rightly should take in all of the time since the Sun of Righteousness withdrew His physical presence, for it has been dark all over the world since He left the earth.

The disciples were on the sea. The sea can be very inviting and yet very unpredictable and treacherous. It can be calm today and violent tomorrow. The sea bears its cargoes in peace and tranquility today, but tomorrow it will dash them into the murky depths. For the disciples that night, Galilee was a contrary, troubled, restless sea—disturbed, turbulent, treacherous, cruel, potentially deadly.

In the Scriptures, the world of humanity is sometimes metaphorically referred to as the sea. Indeed, humankind is not unlike the sea I have just described. The leaders of the nations meet at conference tables, shake hands and toast one another. They have their pictures taken together. Outwardly they laugh and joke as if in friendship. But the next day these men are enemies again, and they would kill each other if given a chance. We live in a turbulent, cruel, treacherous world.

Contact without merging

Even the relationship of the ship to the sea is illustrative. It was a relationship of contact without merging. That ought to be the relation of the church to the world. The world is real, and the Christian church is here in this world for a purpose. Thank God, we are on top of the "sea." We maintain the same relation to the world as did that little ship to the Sea of Galilee. It is contact without merging.

Our problem is the same one the disciples faced. The sea is always trying to get into the ship—the world is always trying to get into the church. The world around us continues to try to find its way in, to splash in, to come in with soft words and beautiful white crests, forever whispering, "Don't be so aloof; don't be so hostile. Let me come in. I have something for you—something that will do you good!" The world is making offers to the church, but the church does not need the world! The world has nothing that the Christian church needs.

Granted, there is the sense of need we have because we are human beings and citizens. I get my food through the efforts of farmers and ranchers, I travel the highways of our nation, I depend upon police and firemen. And so do you. But that is another thing altogether. Even in those matters, we are not merging; we are in contact without merging.

Some people say they are helped in their faith through the offerings of science and the answers of education. I have a little book in my study (I use it for a window prop when I want to get more air) that has chapters entitled, "Finding God through Science," "Finding God through Nature," "Finding God through Art." Why should we be trying to find God through a back door? Why should we always be peering out of some cellar window looking for God when the whole top side of the building is made of sheer crystal and God is shining down—revealed? We need to open the skylights of our hearts, look up and invite God in.

I am sure the disciples were busy bailing on that wildly stormy night, trying to keep the water out of their boat. It was a question of survival. And, whether we believe it or not, it is a question of survival with the church of Jesus Christ today! It is not enough to lean back on our forebears and say with the first-century Jews, "We have Abraham to our father." John the Baptist told them, "And now also the axe is laid unto the root of the trees: therefore every tree which bringeth not forth good fruit is hewn down, and cast into the fire" (Matthew 3:9-10).

Denominations do not count

The living God is not worried about our denominations and our churchly traditions. He is not pledged to preserve our religious family trees. He only wants to get the world evangelized. God is not concerned about preserving any of our Christian denominations, but He is concerned about the life of the church of Jesus Christ—the spiritual church, regardless of what she may call herself. Our Lord is concerned that the church of Jesus Christ should be saved from the incoming waves. A little of the world here, a little there—these move in on the church until the time comes when we no longer have a spiritual church. Instead, we have a sinking vessel.

For the disciples in the boat, their intention was to cross to Capernaum. For them, Capernaum was home. The disciples were in the ship on their way home, and it was night. In our day, the church of Jesus Christ is on her way home, still toiling, still rowing, and it is night.

When we think about the church, the real church of Jesus Christ, some of us hold such an ideal picture in our minds that it is hard to be realistic about the toiling and the rowing. We think of the church in idealistic terms—fixed up and garnished and made beautiful in all ways.

But those disciples in the boat were not idealists; they were realists. They smelled of the sea. Their language was not schooled and academic. They were plain men who were sailing home. Their situation was not a perfect one and their talk was not necessarily about sacred themes. They may have argued. One or two may have sulked. Someone perhaps went to sleep and did not pull his weight. But they were all sailing home together, and Jesus was on the mountain praying for them all.

So it is today in the church of Jesus Christ. There are still disagreements among the people of God. There were in Paul's day, and there are now. There are many imperfections among us. There are existing conditions that ought not to be there—but they are. On the sea that night long ago, the disciples were tired, weary, sleepy, homesick—sailing for Capernaum and home. Their situation was not ideal. They were still in human circumstances. But they were the apple of our Lord's eye. He loved them, and He prayed for them.

We await Jesus' coming

"And it was now dark," the Scriptures say, "and Jesus was not come to them" (John 6:17). For the church of Jesus Christ, it was dark in the first and second centuries, and Jesus did not come. It was dark in the days of Constantine, it was dark when Bernard of Clairvaux lived, it was dark when Martin Luther preached. It was dark when John Wesley stood on the tombstone to preach, it was dark when George Fox walked the hills and vales of England. And in all that time Jesus did not come. It is *still* dark, and we still wait. We do not want to admit that we are disappointed, but we are, nevertheless!

As the wind rose and the tempest in its fury tossed their ship, no doubt the disciples on the Sea of Galilee cried out, "Where are you, Lord?" And the church of Jesus Christ, caught in a moral tempest that threatens to tear it apart, makes the same plea. Thank God, we have Christ's assurance that "the gates of hell shall not prevail against" (Matthew 16:18) His church. Churches may die, but *the* church still lives. The church of Jesus Christ, composed of all the people of God, shall never perish!

I remind you that Jesus Christ is still Lord. He is still the head of His Body, the church. We do not have to apologize for Him. He does not want us to soften His gospel to make it more acceptable to the world. He is not looking for us to defend Him, to argue on His behalf. His eyes see through the darkness. He hold the church in the hollow of His hand even while it is being tossed on the wild sea.

And just as He left the mountain at the proper time, miraculously walking on the water to join His struggling disciples, so He will return from heaven to gather us up and bring us home. He is not here yet, but He is coming! We do not know when He will come within hailing distance, but we know He will come at just the right time. His love and His keen interest in His people will not permit Him to remain away longer than necessary.

Let us not be fearful. The Savior is walking on the sea. He is coming our way. Though it is dark and the winds blow strong, our little ship is on its way Home!

Titles by A.W. Tozer available through your local Christian bookstore: